Timothy McLean

TXM Lean Solutions Pty. Ltd., Australia

GROW YOUR FACTORY, GROW YOUR PROFITS

LEAN FOR SMALL AND MEDIUM-SIZED MANUFACTURING ENTERPRISES

CRC Press
Taylor & Francis Group
Boca Raton London New York

CRC Press is an imprint of the
Taylor & Francis Group, an **informa** business

A PRODUCTIVITY PRESS BOOK

CRC Press
Taylor & Francis Group
6000 Broken Sound Parkway NW, Suite 300
Boca Raton, FL 33487-2742

© 2015 by Taylor & Francis Group, LLC
CRC Press is an imprint of Taylor & Francis Group, an Informa business

No claim to original U.S. Government works

Printed on acid-free paper
Version Date: 20141020

International Standard Book Number-13: 978-1-4822-5585-0 (Paperback)

Visit the Taylor & Francis Web site at
http://www.taylorandfrancis.com

and the CRC Press Web site at
http://www.crcpress.com

For Katerina, Raisa, and Zoya

Contents

4 Make Your Product Flow: Redesign Your Process....................33

5 Getting the Right Layout and Equipment.............................51

6 Developing an Organizational Structure and the Leadership to Sustain It 67

Foreword

If you are running a small to medium-sized enterprise (SME) and feel increasingly surrounded by growing issues—longer lead-times, no time for product development, and working longer hours, to name but a few—then this book is for you. If you have heard about Lean, maybe read a couple of books about it, even been to some presentations from "Lean experts" yet somehow cannot see how—or find the time—to apply it in your business, then this book is definitely for you.

I first met Tim McLean more than 10 years ago when he worked for a large global company called PPG. He was passionate about wanting to improve performance in the operation he ran and a keen advocate for applying Lean to do this. Tim's career and Lean journey had not been the traditional pathway through industrial engineering and big automotive companies. Rather, Tim was a chemical engineer who had spent a couple of decades adapting Lean techniques to the factories he managed. These were all small to medium-sized operations in industries such as packaging, printing, and plastics that had little in common with the automotive assembly line. As a result Tim (like myself) was fascinated by the challenges of finding the best ways to apply the powerful Lean approach in "nontraditional" applications and for smaller operations.

At the time I met Tim, I was being sponsored by the Victorian government to come to Australia to do two things: to present at a manufacturing conference and to work with a High Performance Consortium (HPC) that was run by two friends of mine, Hugh O'Donnell and Carla Geddes. We discussed how I might help their clients, which were mostly small to medium-sized companies in Victoria, Australia. I was not sure how to do this as I usually only worked with large global companies that had lots of resources and specialists. My approach in helping them apply Lean principles was to run 5-day rapid improvement workshops. None of the companies in the HPC could afford the time or the resources to support a full-time 5-day workshop. As the operations director at one of the larger members of the consortium, Tim offered to host the workshop and suggested a compromise approach. He had a problem in his material warehouse—to put it bluntly, it was a mess in terms of both housekeeping and poor picking performance. A few people from each HPC member company worked together to figure out how to run the material warehouse better based on Lean principles plus cut the time from 5 to 3 days. I condensed my approach into just 3 days. We used his suggested approach and it was a big success that people still remember and talk about. For Tim, the workshop further reinforced his belief that while Lean principles could indeed help small to medium-sized companies improve their performance and profitability, there were two fundamental barriers to this happening. First, most, if not all, Lean books, consultants (like me), and teachings are geared toward helping large, often global companies. Second, and more importantly, the senior people in small to medium-sized companies (often the owner of the business) frequently performed multiple roles and were under tremendous time pressure. They needed a different approach if they were to successfully learn about Lean and apply it in their business.

For Tim it was both a challenge and an opportunity—one where he could put his considerable abilities, experience, and people skills to good use helping people in small to medium-sized businesses solve their issues and problems. Such was his conviction on this that he resigned from PPG and, with some inspiration and good advice from Hugh O'Donnell of HPC and others, started his own small company focused solely on this need. In 2009, Tim partnered with Anthony Clyne, a leading Australian Lean coach with a wealth of experience in applying Lean thinking in diverse areas such as food processing, jobbing shops, services, and automotive, and together they formed TXM Lean Solutions.

During the next 10 years, Tim, Anthony, and their growing team at TXM have worked with hundreds of owners and leaders in small to medium-sized businesses from a huge range of manufacturing industries to understand their issues, concerns, and needs. Tim and his team have been extremely successful in helping these businesses identify appropriate Lean approaches to address these challenges before supporting them in implementation. As a result, Tim has a wealth of experience—and some great examples of success—in both the needs of small to medium-sized businesses and how to address these in order to grow the business and increase profits. This book captures all of this knowledge. If you are an owner or senior leader struggling with numerous issues and problems in trying to manage a small to medium-sized business yet not quite being able to figure out how to improve your situation, then I encourage you to read this book—it will help you. I wish you the best of luck!

Ian Glenday
Repetitive Flexible Supply Ltd.
Bath, United Kingdom

Acknowledgments

There are many people who I would like to acknowledge for their support in writing this book. First, I would like to thank my wife, Katerina, for her proofreading and sound advice on the book and her tolerance in putting up with my obsession with manufacturing and factories for the past 25 years. My editor, Martin Smith, provided invaluable assistance in helping improve the book, making it more readable, motivating me to complete it, and providing me with insight into how to structure the material.

Apart from the writing of the book, I would like to thank the people who inspired it. In particular, I thank my business partner, Anthony Clyne. Anthony is (in my opinion) the best practical Lean coach I have ever seen, and almost all the impressive Lean transformation case studies referred to in this book (including Branach, Larnec Doors, and Sykes Racing) were the result of his coaching. The other members of the TXM team also all inspired and educated me in the secrets of creating sustainable Lean transformation in small and medium-sized companies, and for this I thank them.

The biggest inspirations, however, are the companies themselves. I am particularly grateful to Mike Walsh from Branach, Jeff Lawrence from Sykes Racing, Phil and Leon Joyce from Larnec Doors, and Michael Plarre from Ferguson Plarre for their generous support of TXM over several years. These companies have opened their doors to dozens of other companies looking to learn from their experience and have also allowed us to share their case studies more broadly through blogs, articles, videos, and this book. Beyond these companies, every one of the dozens of companies we have worked with over the past decade is inspiring in its own way. It is really tough to run a successful manufacturing business in the twenty-first century. The hours are long, the risks high, the competition fierce and unrelenting, and the rewards often inadequate. These businesses often survive through the passion and perseverance of their owners who are all to be congratulated for the contribution they make to their employees, their communities, and their country. If our work at TXM and this book help some of these passionate entrepreneurs to gain a competitive edge, improve their returns, and make their lives a little bit more rewarding and less stressful, then we will have achieved our most important mission.

About the Author

Tim McLean is founder and managing director of TXM, one of the Asia Pacific's leading Lean consulting companies. Tim was first introduced to Lean and Operational Excellence in the late 1980s as a young production manager of a small plastics extrusion plant, part of German global chemical manufacturer, Hoechst AG. Tim went on to lead a range of medium-sized manufacturing plants across the plastics molding, packaging, printing, and chemical industries for major companies, including Hoechst AG, Amcor, and PPG. Tim was fortunate to be coached by a succession of mentors steeped in the principles of Lean. As an operations manager and general manager, Tim then faced the real challenge of applying these theories to drive performance in his plants.

After a successful 16-year career leading manufacturing operations, Tim turned down a transfer to Europe in order to set up TXM, a consulting business in Australia aimed at helping other manufacturing leaders like himself achieve their goals. TXM has since grown to be one of the leaders in Lean in Asia and the Pacific, operating from offices in Australia and China and carrying out projects with small, medium, and large manufacturers throughout the region. In line with Tim's experience and values, TXM has developed a reputation for delivering practical outcomes for manufacturers, especially SMEs. It is this experience that Tim has drawn on in writing *Grow Your Factory, Grow Your Profits.*

Tim and TXM have an extensive network throughout the Asia Pacific region, and Tim is a frequent speaker at industry events, including the Association for Manufacturing Excellence Conferences, Lean Enterprise

China, the International Society of Pharmaceutical Engineers, Australian Manufacturing Week, and many more. TXM has a weekly blog (www.txm.com.au/blog) to which Tim is a major contributor, and Tim's quarterly e-newsletter goes out to more than 2,000 manufacturing leaders around the region (www.txm.com.au/resources/newsletters). Tim also provides articles to a wide range of manufacturing industry publications, including *Australian Manufacturing Technology, Manufacturers Monthly, Australia-China Connections, China Sourcer Magazine*, etc. Examples of these articles can be found at www.txm.com.au/resources/articles.

Tim and TXM have a strong social media presence, primarily on LinkedIn, with over 1,000 connections, three groups (Australian Manufacturing Futures, Total Excellence Manufacturing, and Lean Support China), and regular and popular contributions to Lean interest groups across the globe. TXM also actively promotes its content via Twitter, Facebook, and a YouTube Channel (TXMLeanVideo).

Contact Tim McLean at info@txm.com.au

Introduction: About This Book

This book is designed to give you a start-to-finish guide for how to run a successful small or medium-sized (SME) manufacturing operation. If you are a start-up business or have just become involved in manufacturing, I recommend you read it from start to finish. However, each chapter is designed as a stand-alone mini-guide on the chapter topic; therefore, you can also choose to read just the chapters relevant to you and the issues you face.

There is a seemingly inexhaustible supply of books about manufacturing; you will find tens of thousands of them listed on Amazon.com alone. From my experience, however, a great many of them make assumptions about your business that hold true only if you are working in a large company. What if your business does not have a separate production engineering department, a training department, or even a human resources department?

If this last sentence describes your company, you are probably in the same category as the overwhelming majority of manufacturers on the planet. You can consider yourself an SME, which, defined loosely, is a company employing fewer than 500 people and turning over less than $200 million in sales from a single manufacturing site. Within this group, one could probably define small manufacturers as those turning over less than $5 million per year and employing fewer than 30 people. These definitions are a bit arbitrary, and I have set the revenue and headcount cutoffs a bit higher than the government statisticians would; however, in my experience, a plant employing 30 people has more in common with a plant employing 15 people than with one employing 100 people, and a plant employing 500 people (especially in Asia) will have more in common with one employing 200 people than with one employing 2,000 people.

Your business will likely be privately or family owned, but equally it could be a small cap listed company or a plant within a larger corporation. I believe the principles within this book apply equally to all these categories.

Chapter 1

One Size Does Not Fit All

What You Will Learn in This Chapter

- How small and medium-sized enterprises (SMEs) differ from big companies and why the approach to improvement should be different
- The life cycle of small and medium-sized manufacturers and why an effective production system based on Lean is essential for sustained profitable business growth

What Is Different about a Small to Medium-Sized Manufacturing Company?

Apart from its size, there are a number of factors that make a small to medium-sized manufacturing enterprise different. First, it is likely that the person with overall responsibility for leading the site will have a direct personal connection with everyone working in the plant, as well as a close connection with the company's top executives. That person's title will probably be one of the following: manufacturing manager, plant manager, general manager, or operations manager. For purposes of this book, we will call him or her the "manufacturing manager."

It is also likely that the manufacturing manager will have responsibilities, that range increasing as the size of the manufacturing operation decreases. Staff roles are also likely to be combined in the SME. For example, Human Resources (HR) might handle safety and training as part of the HR role (assuming there is an HR function), while the responsibility for process improvement might be folded within the Quality function or be a direct responsibility of the manufacturing manager.

In the typical SME, money is tight. The result is that SME manufacturers often lack access to resources that large manufacturers routinely have at their disposal, and therefore the SME's approach to implementing change needs to be altered to reflect this reality. For stand-alone manufacturing operations (not part of a large corporate organization), SME manufacturing managers do not have the ability to call on established corporate expertise, standards, methods, and benchmarks. The SME manufacturing manager needs to figure it out for him- or herself.

Small to medium-sized operations are also, in our experience, different in regard to the types of products they manufacture. They are generally not engaged in mass production such as large factories operating in low-cost economies. And the plant is unlikely, for example, to engage in very large, complex products such as automotive assembly or civilian jet aircraft. Generally speaking, SMEs are also not involved in heavy continuous process manufacturing such as smelting and petrochemicals.

Increasingly, SMEs are likely to produce a complex range of highly customized and highly engineered products. Those products might be delivered to a local market, leveraging local service, or they might be aimed at a global or regional product niche such as specialized machine tools or specialized electronics. Production is usually in short runs and frequently make-to-order. SME process* manufacturers will generally produce in batches or short runs and frequently have a complex product range to manage. While this is a generalization—and TXM does work with SMEs involved in mass production or companies with narrow product lines—they are becoming the exception. The trend is toward increasing complexity, low volume, and custom manufacturing. This is occurring even in process industries such as food manufacturing, coatings manufacturing, and packaging. Unfortunately, most of the books and articles I have read on the subject assume that the plant is involved in mass production such as automotive manufacturing or consumer electronics. It is then left to the SME reader to interpret how to apply the tools and methods of large manufacturing to the SME world.

As an operations and general manager of a number of small to medium-sized manufacturing plants before starting TXM, I experienced firsthand the

---

* I use the term "process manufacturing" to describe batch or continuous process production such as food, coatings, pharmaceutical, plastics, and packaging manufacturing. This is opposed to "discrete manufacturing" where output is in discrete units such as cars, boats, or caravans.

challenges of managing complex product ranges and short-run production and had to figure it out for myself. No longer. *In our consulting practice, we have had a decade of implementing Lean and operational excellence for small to medium-sized manufacturers. As a result, we have learned how to adapt big-company, mass-production Lean manufacturing principles to work for complex SME manufacturing. And we have turned SMEs into high-performance manufacturing organizations.* This book describes what we learned and how you can apply those same valuable lessons to your SME.

Branach Manufacturing: The Story of a Manufacturing SME

To understand how this might relate to your business, it is good to relate it to a real example. Branach Manufacturing in Melbourne, Australia, is a great example of the typical challenges small and medium-sized manufacturers face when they try to grow.

A little over 20 years ago, Branach Manufacturing founder Mike Walsh applied for a graduate engineering role at a composites manufacturing business. Mike missed landing the job but became fascinated by composites and their potential, and started to think about products he could design using composite materials. The result was a unique design for an extension ladder (Figure 1.1).

Composites have been widely used for ladders in professional applications due to their strength, light weight, and excellent electrical insulating properties. However, the commercially available ladders were all made from a fiberglass C-section, which tended to lack rigidity, thus resulting in composite ladders that lacked stability and were prone to damage. The last thing a linesman needed when climbing 10 meters up a power pole was a wobbly ladder. Mike realized that a box section or rectangular section would be better, but the challenge was how to fit the rungs into a box section. After a lot of careful design and trials, Mike developed a system that worked; it enabled rungs to be securely fixed in between two vertical composite box sections. He patented this design and Branach Manufacturing was born.*

Mike found a ready market with electricity utilities and emergency services, who were the first to see the benefits of Branach's safer, more stable extension ladder. Branach offered a further point of differentiation by customizing

---

* Visit www.branach.com.au

Figure 1.1 Branach access platforms in use for helicopter maintenance.

ladders to meet specific customer needs. For example, one electricity utility required that the rungs of the ladder be made of fiberglass as well, while a major fire service wanted a special latching mechanism so ladders could be more quickly extended. Mike and his team developed additional safety features and then had another breakthrough when Branach developed a range of A-frame access platforms. These lightweight, ingenious, and extremely safe access platforms gave users a simple, mobile, and effective way to work at heights of up to six meters (19.6 feet). The initial use was for stock picking. Major distribution centers soon became buyers, and other applications soon emerged, such as maintenance access ladders for aircraft and helicopters. A national distribution deal with Australia's largest industrial products distributor started to drive sales, and soon interest was coming from markets around the world.

At this point when sales were really starting to move, Branach had grown to a team of around 25 people, and Mike could see the potential to grow his business even larger. However, there was a problem: the Branach factory could not keep up with sales demand. Lead-times expanded to 6 weeks for customized products. A talented engineer, Mike was spending much of his time expediting jobs to meet customer demands. There was certainly no time to think about product development and business growth. The business was constantly running out of key materials, thus leading to more production delays, which in turn demanded frequent expediting. The company was also running out of space, forcing Mike to rent the building across the road from the plant. Finally and critically, the machine that Mike had developed to insert the rungs into the vertical box sections was struggling to keep up with demand and regularly breaking down.

Because of all these problems and inefficiencies, overhead and labor costs were rising. Housekeeping was terrible. The business was no longer profitable, and Mike was certainly no longer enjoying the business he had worked so hard to create.

Mike started to look for a better way. Fortunately at the time, Melbourne had a government-funded program (based on one developed in Toronto, Canada) that enabled manufacturers to visit noncompeting companies and learn from their experiences. It was during one of these visits that Mike and I met. About 12 months later, Mike gave me a call. The challenge Mike gave us was to help him get his factory into shape so it could support the growth of his business. I will tell you the end of the Branach story at the conclusion of the final chapter of this book, so if you hate suspense, then skip to Chapter 12; otherwise read on. This book describes what Mike and other SME executives did to significantly improve the operations of their companies.*

How You Might Have Arrived at Where You Are—And How to Move Forward

Mike Walsh's story is typical of almost every SME manufacturer I see. Most manufacturing businesses start with a great idea. Typically, the owner (or

---

* You can view an interview with Mike Walsh from Branach Manufacturing at http://txm.com.au/video/txm-video-lean-case-study-branach-manufacturing

parent company) invents a great new product or spots a potential new market opportunity for an existing product. Initially, sales are slow, and lots of businesses fail at this point; but then the business identifies a group of customers that represents the right market for the product, finds effective marketing techniques to let those customers know about the product, and sales start to take off. At this point the business is sustainable, successful, and probably quite profitable. As sales volumes increase, the number of employees in the factory starts to increase. The complexity of the business increases with more products, more customers, and more employees. Managers are employed to spread the workload previously handled by the owner and, as a result, overhead increases.

However, as the owner or manufacturing manager, you will find at some point that something is going wrong. You spend more and more of your time expediting and juggling priorities to keep customers happy. Revenue keeps increasing but profits do not keep pace. More and more of your cash is tied up in inventory. You might be running out of plant space but your plant is chock-full of material and parts and incomplete orders. The key leaders in a business like this spend the overwhelming majority of their time focused on just getting today's orders out the door and firefighting daily issues. As a result, they do not have any time to think about strategy, product development, marketing, and the things that will continue to drive the growth of the business. Managers and business owners in this situation tend to work very hard and do not get much satisfaction from their work. It is often highly stressful and frustrating, and the rewards in terms of profits are very small. It is at this point that many of our customers call TXM and ask for help. Usually, this occurs at around $5 million revenue or 30 employees. This is often the point at which the transition from a small-sized manufacturer to a medium-sized manufacturer begins.

But what if you don't get help? If you don't change direction at that crucial point when the problems I just mentioned become apparent, then your people and your processes will eventually become overloaded, *even if you attempt to solve the problem by adding more and more managers and planners or expensive ERP (enterprise resource planning) software.* In fact, at some point, you will find that adding more people simply adds to the confusion. Once you reach overload, lead-times blow out and you start missing customer delivery dates. Inventory buildup hampers cash flow, and you start to write off more and more slow-moving and obsolete stock. As problems multiply, you find yourself becoming more and more frustrated with your key staff and they with you, so you start "turning over" managers and employees at a rapid rate. This instability translates into increasing scrap and rework, higher warranty costs, and customer product returns that you never would have made when your business was smaller and you had full control over operations. Eventually, customers will have had enough, and you start to lose orders and your business goes into rapid decline. If you are lucky, you might get to sell out in a fire sale before you plunge into bankruptcy.

Hopefully your business is nowhere near the end of the cycle I have described, but you are understandably apprehensive about your company failing. Fortunately, this situation can be turned around, although the longer you hesitate to reverse the deterioration, the more difficult it will be to make substantial improvements in time to save the company.

Most likely, the element missing from your business is an effective production system. By a production system I mean all the processes, systems, and procedures needed to ensure that you can deliver the right product to your customer at the right cost at the right time, every time, and every day. This system needs to encompass

- How you manage customer demand
- How you measure and improve factory performance
- Your production flow and plant layout
- Your organizational structure, and how you select and develop your people
- How you manage materials
- How your people are managed
- How you make improvements and lock them in

Each of these topics is a key element of an effective production system, and a chapter in this book discusses each one. Implement all these elements successfully and you will build a platform for the rapid and sustainable future growth of your business.

After 25 years of working in manufacturing in a huge range of industries, I firmly believe that Lean manufacturing (also known as the Toyota Production System) is the most practical and effective basis for the development of a production system ever developed. Therefore, the principles outlined in this book all derive from the Toyota Production System and are adapted based on our experience working with more than 100 small and medium-sized manufacturing companies during the past decade.

Chapter 2 explains a bit more about the Toyota Production System and why a system used by such a big company (i.e., Toyota) is so effective when applied to improving SME manufacturers. However, first let's explore what makes SME manufacturers special, and what some of the things are that differentiate them from big companies.

What Large and SME Manufacturing Managers Can Learn from One Another

At TXM we find a lot of interesting techniques and methods that big-company and SME manufacturing managers can share with one another. Here are some of the best ideas:

The Top Five Things That Big Companies Can Learn from Small Companies

These are things that big corporations often forgot as they grew:

1. **They focus on the customer:** SMEs never forget that it is the customers who pay the bills. Most employees have direct contact with customers, and company owners tend to think a lot about what their customers want and the best way to deliver it. The best companies live in their customers' operating reality, so the people who build rowboats row them and the people who make campers sleep in them.
2. **They have fewer meetings:** Typically, managers in big companies spend at least half their days in meetings. Many meetings are poorly run, with no agenda, no effective chairperson, no time limit, and few outcomes; and if there are outcomes, there is little or no follow-up. Small manufacturers cannot afford to sit around in meetings. They tend to have short, focused discussions, often standing up in the office area or shop floor rather than sitting down in a boardroom remote from the action of the production floor.
3 **They never stop innovating:** We are constantly amazed by the ability of small manufacturers to innovate. It seems that SME manufacturers are constantly looking for new ideas, new products, and new ways of doing things to drive growth. Often in big companies there is a tendency to rest on one's laurels with successful products, innovate only reactively to competitors' products, and spend most of the time reducing costs (not a bad thing, but the wrong focus when their primary need is for improved products and superior customer service).

4. **They lead by example:** Successful private business owners usually have little management training and limited time to read books about manufacturing, but they frequently inspire great loyalty in their staff because they are passionate about their businesses, their customers, their products, and their employees. While they are often tough and demanding bosses, they value good employees, and they never expect their employees to do something they have not done or would not do (because, in many cases, they have worked their way up from making the product on a kitchen table or on the production floor).

5. **They ensure stable leadership and planned succession:** For many private business owners, succession is a key issue, whereas it often gets only lip service in bigger companies. The SME chief executive tends to plan far in advance for who will succeed him and then grooms that person (often the next generation in the family) to take the reins. This is a surprisingly difficult task, one not to be underrated, but done well it leads to stable leadership succession. It means that initiatives such as Lean manufacturing have time to take hold and be sustained from one generation of leadership to the next. In big companies, senior management turnover and ambition rule, which means a new leader every 2 years with new ideas and little interest in continuing the initiatives of his predecessors.

While these are valuable ideas that big companies can learn from SMEs, we often find that we need to teach SMEs some big-company rigor as part of their introduction to Lean manufacturing.

The Top Five Things that SMEs Can Learn from Their Big Brothers

These are the things that your business will need to develop as it grows:

1. **They standardize practices:** A common success factor that enables an organization to grow larger is the ability to share what it has learned. Whether it is the knowledge of what constitutes 11 different herbs and spices to coat fried chicken or the best way to disperse pigments in paint resins, the ability to take practices from one location and replicate them successfully in another location is critical to growing a small business into a big business. *Big companies are good at documenting what they do to lock in knowledge and share it. The*

failure to do this is a key reason why smaller companies do not grow. Critical technical and managerial knowledge resides in a few individuals, undocumented, and therefore not shareable with others.

2. **They understand what makes them great:** Great corporations have an innate sense of the factors that make the business successful. These are often woven into the culture of the company in the "way things are done around here," and shared with everyone in the business. Often, SME leaders are too busy to reflect on the secrets of their success and therefore allow those critical success factors to be lost without realizing it. In other cases, critical success factors rely on the founders' expertise and are lost when those founders leave their companies. This can happen even in very large companies; Apple and News Corp., for example, are companies that appear to be struggling without the inspiration of their founders.

3. **They get the structure right and assign responsibility:** An efficient big company is a like a well-organized football team. Everyone knows his position and plays it, and players support each other as needed. Sometimes small companies can be like children playing football—everyone crowding around the ball and nobody in position. The ball is metaphorically today's crisis. Big companies generally have structure; jobs and responsibilities are well defined, and performance feedback and staff development are highly methodized. This ensures that employees know where they stand, have a career path, and know their jobs. SME roles are often less clearly defined, and less focus is given to developing a well-rounded staff. As a result, turnover is often higher, resulting in issues arising where responsibilities are not clear.

4. **They know the balance sheet matters as much as the profit-and-loss statement:** *Most SME business owners focus on profit, while most large companies focus on return on shareholders' funds.* This is driven by the demands of the share market. Translated: big companies are often as focused on minimizing capital as they are on maximizing returns. SMEs, on the other hand, frequently lack discipline in managing inventory and other forms of working capital, and that translates into higher debt and lower returns. A Lean manufacturing approach creates breakthrough reductions in inventory and increases the productivity of fixed assets.

5. **They understand that planning is essential:** Big businesses are usually good at planning. They routinely develop formal plans across the broad spectrum of business functions. Major projects are often carefully planned, and business risks are assessed and mitigated. There

is usually broad consultation about major initiatives and changes in direction. On the other hand, SMEs frequently fail to plan thoroughly enough. They often live day to day and do not take time to assess the direction of their business in terms of finance, marketing, human resources, and operations. Decisions are often reactive because everyone is so busy fighting fires. *However, no company, big or small, can afford **not** to plan.* Big companies also recognize that when they set strategic objectives, they need to support them with resources and expertise. Both internal and external resources (such as consultants) are marshaled behind the key strategic goals and projects of the business. SMEs often develop good strategies and goals but fail to direct adequate resources behind those goals and projects, thus resulting in goals not achieved and projects not delivered effectively.

Key Points in Chapter 1

- SME manufacturers include the overwhelming majority of manufacturing plants in the world. This book focuses on their needs.
- SME manufacturers tend to have "flatter" organizations with fewer functional departments and resources than big companies.
- Managers in SMEs tend to wear multiple hats and are extremely busy.
- Senior leaders in SMEs often have a close connection to all their people and can lead change very directly.
- A lack of good business processes and standardization often hinders the ability of SMEs to grow and compete effectively.
- In order to grow, an SME manufacturer needs to develop an effective "Production System"—all the processes, systems, and procedures needed to ensure that you can deliver the right product to your customer at the right cost at the right time, every time, every day.
- The Toyota Production System or Lean manufacturing is the most effective framework in which to develop a production system for your business.

Chapter 2

What Is Lean Manufacturing, and What Has It Got to Do with Small and Medium-Sized Manufacturers?

What You Will Learn in This Chapter

- A brief history of Lean and how it is relevant to small and medium-sized enterprises (SMEs)
- The concept of value and waste, and how to spot waste in your business that you never knew existed
- The key principles of Lean and why they are important for your business

History and Relevancy of Lean Manufacturing

After World War II, there was a very small car company in a small country town making very bad cars. Most of the employees were former farmers, and the company's production facilities were very basic. The company had major cash flow issues. Like any company in that situation, it lived hand-to-mouth, ordering the exact materials needed to fulfill requirements and trying really hard to assemble the cars quickly, sell them, and use cash from the sales to pay for more raw materials for the next cars on the production schedule.

This is a scenario not uncommon to a lot of struggling small businesses. Most in this situation do not survive, and those that do make sure that they never operate hand-to-mouth again. They order plenty of stock and make sure that they have lots of materials and parts on hand to meet any order that might come along. This presents its own problems of buying excessive quantities of parts and materials.

However, the car company in my story took a different approach. As it crawled its way out of financial stress, it reflected on the experience. Company executives realized that by keeping materials to a minimum and by constantly striving to reduce the cash-to-cash lead-time (from payment of cash for materials to receipt of cash for sales of finished goods) that they could maximize their return and liberate working capital that could then be used to invest and grow, while concurrently providing maximum flexibility to meet customer demands. This company made living hand-to-mouth its way of life. Their executives realized that the important activities in their business were the ones that added value to the product. Those were the activities that customers paid for when they purchased their cars. *They realized, however, that most of what happened in their plants did not add value to the customer, and they defined this as waste and were relentless in trying to eliminate this waste.*

Rather than hand-to-mouth, their way of operating was called *just-in-time*. But they soon realized that operating "just-in-time" gave them little margin for error. The materials and subassemblies had to have perfect quality. Quality had to be ensured at every point in the production and assembly process and in the supply chain. Production machinery had to be reliable and processes consistent, so effective systems for maintenance and for standardizing the work of workers were created.

Gradually, the company built its system of management as it grew. Unlike many companies that focus on holding people accountable for mistakes and hiring and firing, it excelled at learning from its mistakes and developing its employees through this newfound knowledge.

Eventually this very small maker of very bad cars started to grow rapidly. In 2008, it overtook General Motors to become the world's largest car manufacturer, producing around 10 million cars a year in every market of the world. The company I am referring to, of course, is Toyota. And the system of management it developed came to be known as the Toyota Production System. When Western companies realized that they were rapidly losing market share to Japanese manufacturers, a number of US and European academics were sent to study the differences between Toyota and the US and

European manufacturers (most famously Womack and Jones[1]). From these studies the term *Lean manufacturing* was coined to describe Toyota's relentless focus on eliminating waste and lead-time.

I tell this story to illustrate the fact that Lean manufacturing, or the Toyota Production System, was in fact a very practical solution developed by a medium-sized manufacturer to address its cash flow problems. While small manufacturers may be daunted by the size of automotive assembly plants and see them as a unique working environment that has little in common with their business, the reality is that the underlying principles of Lean manufacturing are simple, common sense, and can be applied in *every* manufacturing business, no matter how small.

So, what are those underlying principles?

Value and Waste

As mentioned, Toyota realized that most of what happened in their factories did not add value to the product and therefore was waste. It classified this waste into seven categories. In recent years, others have added more waste categories but I think the original seven is a good place to start. These seven wastes are

1. **Inventory:** Inventory has value on the balance sheet of a company but having more inventory does not add value to your customers. The customer will not pay you more for your product if you hold more inventory, and will also not pay you less if you manage to meet his delivery expectations with less inventory. While inventory will often be necessary (e.g., as a buffer to compensate for variation in customer demand), it should always be considered waste and be minimized.
2. **Waiting Time:** Waiting time is the unproductive time spent by employees waiting for something to happen. Often, they will be waiting for another employee to complete a task or waiting for a machine to complete its cycle. While waiting, the worker is not adding value to the product and therefore waiting is waste.
3. **Motion:** In many tasks, employees will spend a lot of their time walking. Walking from one part of a production line to another, walking back and forth to collect or deliver materials, or walking around their work cells. While walking, employees are not adding value to the customer, so motion is waste.

4. **Transportation:** Closely related to motion is transportation time. This is the time spent moving materials and products around the plant or from location to location—a necessity if you have a large site or multi-site operation, but it does not add value to the product and is therefore categorized as waste.

5. **Defects:** Ask most manufacturing people about waste and they will talk about scrap or defects. Making scrap and defects does not add value to the customers' products and obviously should be considered waste.

6. **Overprocessing:** Production processes frequently incorporate processes that do not add value to the product, and we should consider those processes wasteful and try to eliminate them altogether. Examples of this kind of waste include excessive inspection steps, packaging of work in progress or subassemblies that need to then be unpacked later in the process, and deburring parts (when the drilling or cutting process that caused the burr can be redesigned to prevent the burr in the first place).

7. **Overproduction:** Overproduction is the opposite of just-in-time. Overproduction is producing more than is needed sooner than needed. Overproduction usually manifests itself as work-in-progress inventory. Overproduction is usually caused by big batches and unbalanced processes and is in some ways the worst form of waste as it is associated with increased inventory, more transportation of materials, and often with overprocessing.

Do a Waste Walk

Try training yourself to see waste in your business. Find a place in your plant where you can observe the production process. Turn off your mobile phone and any other distractions and just observe what is happening. Write down each example of waste that you can see.

Now observe a single worker. Time his cycle with your watch and try to see how much time he spends adding value to the product and how much time is spent moving or waiting. Does his process really add value to the customer? Is he producing or overproducing? Write down the examples. Think about why the waste is occurring and what could be done to eliminate it.

Tell the worker what you are doing and ask him what he thinks about your observations and solutions, and what waste reduction ideas he can see in his job. You will find that employees are more than willing to point out ways in which waste can be eliminated, as few enjoy waiting for work or walking back and forth all day. Just by this exercise you are likely to identify waste savings that you can implement immediately. In Chapter 4 we introduce you to a technique that will help you eliminate waste in your whole process: value stream mapping.

Four Rules of the Toyota Production System

Many businesses over the past 30 years have experimented with the tools of Lean manufacturing. Most of you have heard of methods such as 5S, *Kanban*, single minute exchange of die (SMED), and total productive maintenance (TPM).

Despite implementing these tools, many companies did not see the improvements in performance they had expected. Further study of the Toyota Production System revealed some basic principles that supported it. These were described in 1999 in an excellent *Harvard Business Review* article by Spear and Bowen.[2] They identified four rules that were integral to everything Toyota did. Again, these rules are simple, practical, and applicable to every manufacturing business. They are essentially the basic principles that Toyota (and other Lean companies) apply to eliminate the seven wastes. The four rules are

- ■ **Rule 1: All work is specified in terms of content, sequence, timing, and outcome.** This is described as *standard work* and means that, to the extent possible, there is a standard method for every task. This standard work is usually developed with the production team rather than remotely by industrial engineers. It becomes the agreed-upon method that everyone follows to complete a task. As such, it becomes the basis for training employees. *In essence, the standard method means that workers can complete a task and achieve consistent quality outcome in a specified time, every time.* It also provides the basis for improvement. The first question asked by a Toyota improvement coach (or *Sensei*) is always: What is the standard? *They rightfully argue that if you do not have a standard, then you do not know the capability of your current process and therefore you cannot measure improvement or detect deterioration.*

■ **Rule 2: Every customer–supplier connection must be direct, and there must be an unambiguous yes-or-no way to send requests and receive responses in the supply chain.** Every employee at Toyota is a customer and a supplier. Assembly lines are the customers of material handlers, material handlers are customers of parts and materials stores. Each assembly line worker is the customer of the worker upstream of him and the supplier of the worker downstream. Production is the customer of maintenance. Crucially, the team is the customer of the team leader, and the team leaders are customers of their supervisors. In every case, customers and suppliers have clear agreed-upon expectations of supply and response. When an assembly worker empties a bin of parts, it is the job of the material handlers to replenish that bin with another bin of quality replacement parts in an agreed-upon time to ensure that the worker does not run out of needed parts. Each assembly worker has to complete his task in a specified time and to a specified quality and then hand the product on to the next worker on time and without defects. When a worker highlights a problem by pulling his alarm cord (called an Andon cord), the team leader is expected to arrive and support the team member within a specified time. Equally, however, if the worker does not pull the cord, the team leader knows there is not a problem and does not need to offer help to the worker. He can focus instead on other tasks. This clarity greatly simplifies operations. Expectations are clear, and employees are empowered to make decisions and take action based on these simple and clear signals.

■ **Rule 3: The pathway for every product or service is simple and direct.** Every process flow and every business process must be analyzed and unnecessary complexity eliminated. This means that for any given product or part, there is one simple routing rather than many alternative routings. Plant layouts are designed to have a simple end-to-end flow for products and ideally a single production cell where all production steps are completed in one location.

■ **Rule 4: Improvements are made using the scientific method under the guidance of a teacher, at the lowest possible level of an organization.** When we study science or engineering in school or at the university, we learn the scientific method. Problems are solved by analyzing the root causes, developing hypotheses, performing experiments to test hypotheses, measuring the results of the experiments, and then, if successful, recording and documenting the results and adding them to the body of scientific knowledge. After starting work in business, we usually forget all this. When we have a problem, we usually jump to a solution and tell employees to implement it. Chances are that we know the solution because the problem has happened before (and will happen again), and chances are that we will just address the symptoms of the problem (e.g., by reworking defective product) rather than finding the root cause. It is also likely that problems will be handed up the line to managers to solve.

In a Lean production system, we try to apply the Plan–Do–Check–Act (PDCA) cycle. This means that when we have a problem such as a defective product, a machine breakdown, or an excessively long setup, we see this as an opportunity to improve. The team leader, supervisor, or engineer will gather the team to discuss the problem and agree to the most likely root cause (PLAN). Corrective actions will be agreed to and a plan to implement them developed. The corrective actions will then be implemented (DO), and the results tracked over a period of time to make sure that the problem does not occur again (CHECK). If the correction is successful, then standard work will be updated to include the new method, materials, or process that has been developed (ACT). This approach can be painstaking at first, but it means that problems are solved permanently.

About Six Sigma

There is another popular approach to improvement, however, beyond the brief explanation below, I do not discuss it in this book. Some readers may disagree but I do not see it as an effective approach for improving operations in a small or medium-sized manufacturing business. This approach is called Six Sigma or Lean Six Sigma.

There are two key problems with Six Sigma. First, it focuses on variation as the source of waste in processes. Excessive variation is an important source of waste in processes, particularly defects, but it is not the only form of waste. *It's important to understand that you cannot identify and address the majority of the seven wastes through reduction of variation.* This problem is partly addressed by Lean Six Sigma, which aims to incorporate Lean tools within a Six Sigma framework. This is not, however, to dismiss many of the underlying problem-solving tools. They are very good, and we often deploy them as part of Lean projects; however, they are specialized tools and will not provide the full answer for small and medium-sized manufacturers seeking substantial operational improvements.

The second problem with Six Sigma and Lean Six Sigma is the larger problem, and that is the method of deployment. Six Sigma is deployed through a structure of specialist process improvers who are trained to different levels of skill in the improvement techniques. The levels of training correspond to belts, as in the martial arts. Therefore, a Green Belt can lead basic problem-solving activities and simple projects; a Black Belt can train Green Belts, lead more complex projects, and carry out more advanced analysis; and a Master Black Belt can train Black Belts and will generally run the whole Six Sigma program. *In my opinion, this is a resource-hungry, bureaucratic, big-company approach.* It was designed by large bureaucratic companies (GE and Motorola, for example), and I have only seen it work effectively in those companies, and even then, I am skeptical. For small and medium-sized companies, the time, training, and resources required to create a Six Sigma or Lean Six Sigma infrastructure of training and belted specialists are unsupportable.

The other big problem with the deployment approach is that it tends to make problem solving and improvement the job of the specialists rather than every employee's job. In particular, Six Sigma activities often become divorced from key activities and strategic goals of the business and become a burden on line management rather than a support. As one plant manager once told me, "I don't think my budget can afford any more Six Sigma projects." When an improvement effort is seen as costing money rather than saving money, then its usefulness is very limited. In contrast, we will outline an approach to substantial improvements aimed at achieving the most important strategic goals for the business, and which is led and driven by line leadership at every level with the support of specialists as required. That's putting the horse before the cart—not the other way around!

Key Points in Chapter 2

■ Lean manufacturing is not some arcane system developed by big automotive companies for big automotive companies; rather, it is a simple, practical system of business improvement developed originally by a small company that used that approach to become a very big company—Toyota.

- Lean manufacturing defines waste as anything that does not add value to the customer's order. Waste is typically classified into eight categories: transportation, inventory, motion, waiting, overprocessing, overproduction, defects, and underutilized employees. Lean manufacturing is the relentless elimination of that waste.
- Beyond all the fancy visual tools such as *Kanban* cards and 5S, the Toyota Lean manufacturing approach is built on four commonsense principles: (1) standardize the work, (2) make every customer–supplier connection direct and unambiguous, (3) simplify the flow of material and information, and (4) get everyone to solve problems using the scientific method.
- While many of the statistical and problem-solving tools used in Six Sigma are useful, both Six Sigma and Lean Six Sigma are too complex, costly, time consuming, and bureaucratic to be considered effective methods for improving the operations of small and medium-sized manufacturers.

References

1. Womack, J.P., Jones, D.T., and Roos, D. 1990. *The Machine That Changed the World: The Story of Lean Production*. New York: Simon & Schuster/Free Press.
2. Spear, S. and Bowen, H.K. Decoding the DNA of the Toyota Production System. *Harvard Business Review*, September-October 1999, pp. 96–106.

Chapter 3

Deciding Where to Start Your Lean Journey

What You Will Learn in This Chapter

- How to get started on your Lean journey
- The importance of getting your senior management team on board with the change and how to achieve this
- How to identify the cultural and leadership barriers that may block your Lean transformation
- How to select your first Lean pilot project
- Why running a Lean training course for everyone is not the right way to introduce Lean into your business, and will cost you time and money and achieve little
- Why you are "ready" for Lean now

Where *Not* to Start

It would seem pretty logical that the way to start the implementation of Lean in your business would be to train everyone in Lean. There are lots of Lean courses around, and in some countries (such as Australia) there are very generous government subsidies, which make these courses very cheap, or even free. Therefore, why not just choose a training provider and sign up everyone for a course? In our experience, this is a very ineffective, time-consuming, and costly way to get started (even allowing for training subsidies). The aim of training is to impart knowledge, and the outcome is that trainees gain a qualification or certificate to recognize that they have acquired that knowledge. However, knowledge is only useful if it is applied and, in our experience, very few Lean training courses go on to deliver real Lean change. This is because other barriers such as the culture of the organization prevent change from occurring. Also, training a number of people and expecting them to implement improvement tends to, at best, lead to uncoordinated, random, small-scale improvement that will not address the key issues that prevent your business from growing (e.g., the kind of issues Mike Walsh was facing at Branach Manufacturing in Chapter 1).

In fact, the overwhelming majority of SME manufacturers I visit for the first time have already invested considerable time and money in training employees in "Lean" but have achieved no change in their business performance and therefore contact TXM to help them make that change. My advice therefore is to skip the training and go straight to the problems impacting your business.

"Stability First": A Perfect Excuse for Procrastination

Another popular approach is what I call the "stability-first" approach. This approach says that before you can really address the big issues in your business such as long lead-times, high costs, and late deliveries by implementing Lean, you need a foundation of "stability." Essentially, the proponents of this approach say that if your business is facing day-to-day delivery and quality crises, long lead-times and high costs, and has poor processes, it is not "ready" for Lean. Advocates of this approach say you should go away and work on creating "stability" by writing procedures, getting an ISO9001 quality system, writing position descriptions implementing a computerized ERP (enterprise resource plan) system (see Chapter 7 for more on this) before you implement Lean. This approach is a guaranteed recipe for disaster. Not one of these "stability" actions will make a dollar of difference to your bottom line, and an ISO9001 system will not even necessarily improve your quality. In the meantime, the problems of quality, delivery, and cost that are destroying your business are just getting worse. By the time you get around to trying to fix your problems, it may be too late!

If you are facing major problems with quality, delivery, and cost, then I would say that you are just not ready for Lean, and you need to start implementing it *immediately* before things get worse!

There is a basic level of stability that you need. If you plan to make major senior leadership changes (for example, changing the general manager or manufacturing manager), it may be best to wait until this change is completed and the new leadership can take on the project. However, apart from that, my view is that the time to start making major changes is right now. Every day that you wait is costing you money.

First Decide: What Is the Problem We Need to Fix?

Before you even think about doing anything with Lean, you need to define what you want to achieve. What is the problem you are trying to solve, or what are the strategic goals you are trying to achieve? It therefore goes without saying that if your business does not have a clear business plan and business strategy, you need to do this *before* embarking on a process improvement initiative using Lean.

Get the strategy wrong or fail to have a strategy, and I can guarantee that your business will never be successful, no matter how well run your factory is.

Remember that Lean is not a strategy or even a strategic goal. Lean is a means of achieving your strategic goals—it is a means, not an end.

Your strategy will set a vision for your business. It will also set some measurable goals about what you want to achieve in terms of your target markets, new markets that you plan to enter, new products you plan to offer, your target sales level, and the expected rate of growth. That will tell you what you will need to make in the future compared to what you are making now.

The strategy should also identify how the current capabilities of your business compare to the capabilities needed to compete effectively and win market share in your target markets. We call these "capability gaps" and closing these gaps might mean achieving improvements in what you deliver to customers in terms of quality, cost, lead-time, or your ability to respond to changing requirements.

A good example of using Lean to close a capability gap is Larnec Doors in Swan Hill on Australia's Murray River. Phil and Leon Joyce, the Managing Director and Operations Manager of Larnec, respectively, realized that they had a big opportunity to sell their steel personnel doors to a major national building products distributor. However, this distributor was accustomed to buying imported doors from a warehouse with a short lead-time of 4 days. Phil and Leon did not want to build a huge warehouse and invest millions in stock, and they also saw their ability to customize doors as being a key *point of difference with their import competitors, who were less flexible. However, Larnec's lead-time to manufacture and deliver a door was around 2 weeks. Therefore, the challenge for Lean became clear: how to manufacture and deliver a custom-made, make-to-order door in less than 4 days from order. This clear requirement gave a high level of focus on the Lean improvement initiative. The goal of a "4-day door" was achieved in approximately 6 months, and today the business currently delivers doors within 3 days from order.*[*]

Your strategic goals may not be quite as clear and well defined as those at Larnec Doors. However, the more you can define your strategic goals and the capability gaps that you want to address, the greater your likelihood of success. By linking the implementation of Lean to the achievement of strategic goals, you ensure that everyone in your business (particularly your leadership team) can clearly see *why* you are implementing Lean and how the implementation of Lean connects to the future of the business. This will make it more likely that leadership will align its support behind the Lean project. This is because Lean ceases to be "extra work" or a "management initiative," but instead becomes a core activity needed to get the business where it needs to go.

Getting the Key People on Board

We often find that a good place to start with a new Lean implementation project is a Senior Leadership Workshop. This will involve all the key leaders in the business. Typically, this will mean all the direct reports to the CEO and perhaps some or all of the leaders at the next level. It is important that all functions are included, *even those functions that may not initially be directly impacted by the Lean project.* Typically, a Lean project in a manufacturing plant is going to focus first on functions such as production, ordering, purchasing, and warehousing. However, other functions such as sales, engineering, HR (if you have HR), and finance will have a significant indirect impact (and may be directly involved). They need to be fully engaged and aware of the project, its goals, its likely impact, and why it is important to the business. Otherwise they may undermine the project (either inadvertently or deliberately).

---

[*] You can read a more detailed case study about Larnec Doors at http://txm.com.au/case-studies/lean-processes-deliver-quick-order-turnaround

The Senior Leadership Workshop typically will include an introduction to Lean principles (similar to that provided in Chapter 2) and a discussion of how those principles relate specifically to your business. The rest of the workshop can then focus on what the business is hoping to achieve through Lean, the likely barriers to that change (especially leadership and cultural barriers), and how these barriers might be overcome. The workshop can also discuss the likely resource requirements to support the Lean project, short-term impacts that the project may have, and any structural changes that might be necessary to ensure that the Lean project is successful.

If you have good facilitation skills, you may be able to facilitate this workshop yourself or get someone in your team such as the HR manager (if you have one) to facilitate it. I do not recommend this approach. It is much better to get a skilled external Lean consultant to facilitate this workshop. Chapter 12 includes some advice on selecting a good Lean consultant for your business.

Understanding the Barriers to Change

Your strategy should give you some short-, medium-, and long-term goals for what you want to achieve with your Lean project. It should also highlight specific capability gaps that you will need to overcome to achieve your goal, such as Larnec Doors' lead-time problem. However, there are other barriers to change that are less easily measured.

At TXM, we see three main barriers to change through Lean. The first of these is *know-how*: if you do not understand Lean and do not have sufficient knowledge in your business, then you cannot implement it successfully.

Second, *leadership needs to support the Lean transformation*. This is reflected in both words and deeds. As the CEO or manufacturing manager, it is likely that your team and the leaders at other levels will say that they support Lean; however, this is not enough. It will be the behaviors and attitudes that they demonstrate every day that will have the biggest impact on whether the project succeeds or fails. Lean leadership is a big subject, and Chapter 10 provides some ideas on the types of behaviors you and your team will need to adopt. Discuss these behaviors in your Senior Leadership Workshop and how they might work in your business.

Third, *the culture of your business can be a big barrier to change.* These are the assumed attitudes, values, and behaviors that have developed in your business over the years. The culture in an organization does not necessarily change automatically with changes in top leadership; it takes a sustained, consistent effort at every level of leadership to change the culture. Examples of the cultural barriers we encounter include

■ "We always make the monthly numbers"—this may mean we "make the numbers" at the expense of quality and cost.
■ "Make sure you never run out"—this can drive overstocking and excessive batch sizes.
■ "Don't tell me your problems"—this will mean that problems are covered up or temporary fixes are put in place rather than addressing root causes. Employees will tend to suffer in silence rather than report problems that might be costing the business productivity and waste.

There are lots of other examples of cultural values and behaviors that may delay or derail your Lean transformation, but these are some of the most common.

It is long and difficult work to overcome the cultural and leadership barriers to change in your business. However, if you do not overcome them, your Lean transformation will not be sustainable. Your Lean Senior Leadership Workshop provides an opportunity to identify some of the leadership and cultural barriers within your business. I use a simple technique to get the senior leadership team to reflect on their business and highlight the barriers.

I usually ask two questions. First, "What kind of business do we want to be?" Pose the question and get the team members to individually write down as many descriptors as they can think of on sticky notes. When everyone has run out of ideas, get them to stick the ideas on the wall or a whiteboard. Group together similar ideas on the wall. Do you see some common themes? Can you summarize what the group has identified as desirable attributes of your business in the future?

Now pose the second question: "What are the things that prevent us from being the business we want to be?" Repeat the process with the Post-It notes. Do you see common themes again? Focus on highlighting the intangible cultural barriers in your business.

Through this simple exercise you will have also identified some (but probably not all) of the leadership and cultural barriers that you will need to overcome to make the change sustainable. This will enable you and your team to highlight these barriers as you encounter them and take action targeted at overcoming them.

Selecting the First Target for Improvement

You now have some high-level strategic goals and some shorter-term goals that you are hoping to achieve through the implementation of Lean. Your Senior Leadership team has a basic understanding of Lean and how the Lean project should be resourced and structured. You have highlighted some of the key leadership and cultural barriers that might impede change within your business. However, you still do not know where to start your Lean implementation on Day 1. Unless your manufacturing business is very simple (with one product), you will need to further refine the areas that you need to target first. This will ensure that your change is focused and can achieve a reasonable level of change in a short period of time (usually 6 to 12 months).

Your business is likely to make a range of products and operate a range of processes. In Lean we look at your business from the perspective of a customer. Therefore, we look at groups of similar products within your business (your "product families") and follow these product families back through your process to the point where you receive raw materials. We call this process flow for a particular product family a "value stream." The value stream will include all the value-adding steps and the waste involved in processing the raw materials through to finished goods for one product family.

Seeing your business as a collection of value streams is an important change from the way we typically see businesses. Typically we view businesses from above and see a range of functional silos or departments—manufacturing, warehousing, planning, purchasing, logistics, finance, sales, engineering, maintenance. Each of these departments tries to improve its performance independently of the others. Within manufacturing, each process is often its own "silo," for example, machining, welding, painting, and assembly. This often leads to poor outcomes and conflicts as what appears to be an improvement in one department has an adverse impact on another. For example, the machining department might want to make big batches for "efficiency" but this might lead to large inventories of parts and frequent shortages in assembly when parts are not made in time to meet changing customer requirements. The value-stream approach looks at your business horizontally as the customer sees it—in product families. Focusing on value streams means that you will be improving the whole process to benefit your business and the customer, rather than improving one department at the expense of another. It also directs your improvement effort toward the activities that are likely to create the biggest overall improvement rather than achieving localized improvement across the business.

So how do we identify our value streams, and how do we decide which one to focus on? Chapter 4 gives you advice on how to use a product family matrix to identify the different value streams in your business. Our advice is that you then select the value stream that is most important to your business to be the one that you focus on first.

Why Work on the Most Important Value Stream First?

Earlier in my career, I managed an industrial coatings plant. When I was hired, the team had just completed their first Lean manufacturing pilot project. They had chosen a small new product range that ran in an area of the plant outside the main plant building. This was regarded as a safe approach to get the Lean project rolling. The Lean manufacturing team had done a great job, and it really was a fantastic pilot project. However, because it involved a minor product in an obscure corner of the plant, it had almost no impact. When we ran the next pilot, I made sure that the team selected the most important product family in the plant—a range of coatings used for coil steel that represented around 30% of our volume and 25% of our revenue. After we slashed the lead-time and inventory on these products, employees and the business as a whole started to realize that the Lean manufacturing approach could make a big difference in the plant's success, and it was easy to make the case to move on to the next major value stream.

For these reasons, we strongly recommend in most cases that you start by

■ Engaging your Senior Leadership,
■ Defining your strategic goals,
■ Selecting your top-priority value stream, and then
■ Mapping and improving that value stream.

I have discussed a lot about value streams and value stream mapping in this chapter. Therefore, read on to Chapter 4 to learn more about how you can map and improve your value stream.

Key Points in Chapter 3

- Sending everyone to a Lean training course is a costly, time-consuming, and highly ineffective way to implement Lean in your business.
- Before you start implementing Lean, you need to clearly understand why you need to implement Lean and what the strategic goals of Lean are that you are trying to achieve.
- It is important that your leadership team understands and supports your Lean initiative so a Senior Leadership Workshop can help bring them on board.
- Most businesses start by selecting and improving a key value stream in their business.

Chapter 4

Make Your Product Flow: Redesign Your Process

What You Will Learn in This Chapter

- A brief introduction to the powerful Lean technique of value stream mapping.
- How to get started in identifying the value streams within your business, choosing the right value stream to focus on, and developing a current state map
- The key steps involved in developing a future state value stream map for your business
- Key tools and techniques that we find are most effective for SME (small and medium-sized enterprise) manufacturers in implementing their future state

Mapping Your Process with a Value Stream Map

The value stream map is a powerful tool for understanding your business process; it was originally developed by Toyota to help them understand their suppliers and help them improve. When Toyota started sharing their Lean production system with their suppliers through their Supplier Development Team, they discovered that the suppliers operated diverse processes that were very different from automotive assembly. They realized that they needed a tool to analyze the supplier's manufacturing process. Because Toyota was the customer, they were interested in looking at the process from start to finish to understand the value and waste. Toyota realized that to properly understand a process, they needed to map both the processing of the materials as well as the information that controlled the flow of the materials through all the processing steps. Therefore, they developed a tool for mapping their suppliers' processes and called it a "Material and Information Flow" diagram. This is the tool we now call a "Value Stream Map," and it is the best way for you and your team to better understand your process and work out where you need to target improvement. Jim Womack and Dan Jones popularized the term "value stream mapping" in their seminal book, *Lean Thinking*.[1] The definitive how-to guide on value stream mapping, *Learning to See*,[2] was written by former Toyota engineer John Shook. We recommend that you obtain these books if you intend to complete a value stream map of your process, as I will only provide an overview and some key tips and adaptations that we have developed based on our experiences. For more advanced value stream mapping, Kevin Duggan's book, *Creating Mixed Model Value Streams*[3] is also a useful reference.

At TXM, the process steps we use to complete a value stream map are as follows:

- Define the product families. These will be your value streams.
- Select your value stream.
- Select a cross-functional team to analyze the value stream.
- Map the current state to provide an accurate view of how things are now.
- Map the future state. We use a seven-step process to help you and your teams think differently about your process.
- Develop an action plan to implement the future state.
- Implement the future state.

Once the future state is implemented, it becomes your new current state, and you need to consider what your new future state might be.

As mentioned, creating value stream maps is the subject of several books. Therefore, I do not intend to provide a complete "how to do a value stream map guide." Instead, I am going to share with you a few key mapping techniques from our experience, along with some typical future state solutions that apply to SMEs.

Defining Your Product Families

Chapter 3 explained that to define your value streams, you first need to define your product families. But how do you define a product family? In your business, you might already have an idea of what a product family is. For example, in a box plant, it might be all the jobs manufactured using the same die form or the same base print design. In a food plant, it might be all the SKU (stock keeping unit) variants on the same basic product formula. In our value stream mapping process, we have a different (and usually broader) definition of a product family. In this definition, a product family is a group of products that all go through the same or very similar product steps using the same or similar equipment. This typically means all have the same or similar routing.

To determine what your product families are, you need to develop a product family matrix. This lists all your products (or your types of routings in the case of a jobbing shop) down the first column and all your production processes across the top. You then highlight what process each product goes through to see your product families. Table 4.1 shows an example of what a product family matrix might look like for a sheet metal fabrication process.

In the simple example in Table 4.1, you can see that the big and small filing cabinets go through the same set of processes. Therefore, they form a product family. However, you can also see that shelves and toolboxes almost follow the same routing, except that shelves do not require any captive fasteners and toolboxes are not painted. Therefore, we would tend to include toolboxes and shelves in the same product family as the filing cabinets even

Table 4.1   Example of Product Family Matrix

Product	Units per Day	Punch	Laser Cut	Fold	Insert Fasteners	Spot Weld	Weld	Paint	Assemble
Big Filing Cabinet	250		X	X	X	X		X	X
Shelves	150		X	X		X		X	X
Doorjamb	80		X	X				X	
Computer Cabinet	30	X	X	X	X	X	X	X	X
Toolbox	20	X	X	X	X			X	
Small Filing Cabinet	20		X	X	X	X		X	X
Shelf Bracket	20	X	X	X				X	

though they are different products. Likewise, the routings for shelf brackets and doorjambs are similar (shelf brackets need some punching of forms before they are laser cut), so they probably also form a product family.

But be careful; use good judgment. For example, it may be that the assembly process for shelves is completely different and done in a different location than filing cabinets, and they may not sit together well. However, in our experience in sheet metal fabrication, the routing "laser cut-fold-insert-weld-paint-assemble" is very common, and parts that follow this or a similar routing can usually be treated as a single product family. It is also worth noting that the example above is very simplistic. However, even if you make 20 different models of filing cabinet in 15 different colors, they will all be within the same product family if they all follow the same or similar routing.

These product families constitute your value streams and, as suggested in Chapter 3, we will usually start by selecting the most important value stream in your business to work on first.

Current State Mapping Tips

Once you have selected your value stream, you can next create the value stream map. I recommend that you pick up a copy of *Learning to See* to get started on this process. However, some key tips from our experience (once you have read about the basics) are

- Involve all the key employees. Your value stream map should be developed by a team, not an individual, and should involve all the key players along the process from the warehouse supervisor back through production to the purchasing office. Much of the value of current state mapping is to help employees in every department understand the entire process. *We have found this understanding to be lacking even in very small companies with as few as 10 employees.*
- Use real data, not guesswork. It is easy to assemble a group of people to make guesses about your process. You can be almost 100% sure that the guesses will be wrong. Count your inventory, time your processes, and measure your scrap. Just getting out and having a look on the production floor will immediately teach you something about the state of waste in your process. Keep this in mind: if you have the wrong data in your current state map, you will make mistakes in your future state map.

- Start with the customer and work backward in your map, mapping the product flow first and starting again at the customer and mapping the information flow.
- Understand the difference between a process and a step within a process. A new process usually occurs only when the flow of product stops and you need a new piece of information, for example a plan or a *Kanban* card, to move the product to the next step.
- *Always* map the information flow. This includes all the information and communication steps from receipt of the customer order through production planning, purchasing, quality control, and shipping, through to the final dispatch documentation. The information flow is what decides when and how the product will move from step to step through the process. I have seen a lot of companies map the product flow without considering the information that moves the product through that specific process. This misses the whole point of value stream mapping and greatly reduces your opportunity to learn. *Most of the improvement is likely to come through improving the information flow.*
- Avoid branches if you can. Most processes branch off in different directions as you move upstream and through subassembly processes. Avoid including branches in your first version of the map. Focus on the longest and most important product flow and treat subassembly processes like raw material inputs to the main flow.

You should end up with a current state map that looks somewhat like the one in Figure 4.1. You are likely to be shocked by the length of your lead-time and the amount of waste in your process.

What Are We Going to Make?

As discussed in Chapter 3, one of the first questions in our manufacturing business should be: What do we need to make, and how much of it do we need? We use that basic information to determine the rate at which we need to produce product in the plant. We call this rate the "*takt* time." To calculate the *takt* time, take the daily working time in the plant (usually measured in minutes or seconds) and divide it by the number of units you need to produce each day. In our filing cabinet example previously described, we decided that our first product family would be filing cabinets. The plant makes 250 big filing cabinets and 20 small cabinets per day, making the total output 270 per day.

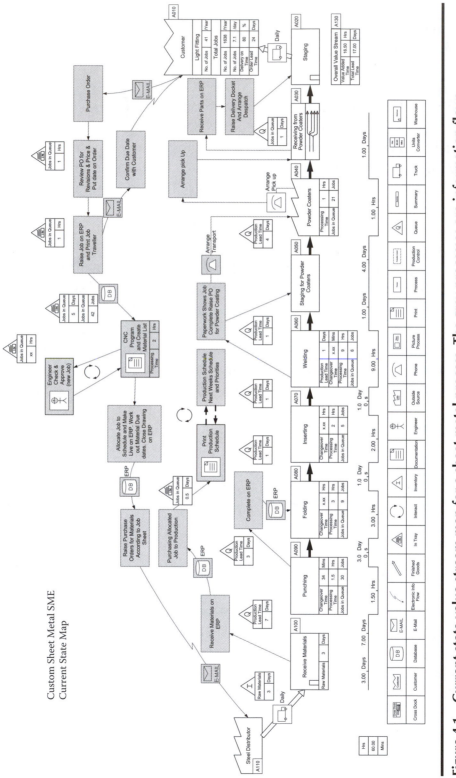

Figure 4.1 Current state value stream map for a sheet metal process. The gray processes are information flows.

The plant works one 8-hour shift per day (480 minutes per day), and the production team takes a 15-minute tea break in the morning, a 30-minute break for lunch, and a 15-minute tea break in the afternoon. This means they have 60 minutes of break time and 420 minutes of productive time per day. Therefore,

$$\text{\textit{Takt} time} = (420 \text{ minutes})/(270 \text{ units})$$

$$= (25,200 \text{ seconds})/(270 \text{ units})$$

$$= 93 \text{ seconds per unit.}$$

In summary, the plant needs to produce a filing cabinet every 93 seconds to meet customer demands.

What Is Your Finished Goods Strategy?

The next step is to decide how you are going to manage your finished goods. We hear executives talk about lots of different finished goods strategies, but in our experience they really all boil down to just two methods: (1) make-to-stock or (2) make-to-order.

In make-to-stock, when a customer places an order, that order goes to your warehouse and a stock picker picks the stock and arranges for it to be shipped to the customer. At some point after that, a signal is sent to production planning to replenish the stock that has just been sold.

The normal situation for a make-to-stock item is that it is available in stock. If it is out of stock, there is a risk that the customer will order the product and your business will be unable to deliver. Therefore, a make-to-stock item with no stock on hand is a problem that must be addressed.

In make-to-order items, when a customer places an order, production planning sends the order to production and they make exactly what the customer needs in the quantity the customer specifies. The production order triggers purchasing or picking of parts or subassembly delivery to the assembly department. In either case, I would consider this make-to-order production. The completed order is then shipped to the customer.

The normal situation for make-to-order is that there is no stock of the product in the warehouse, apart from stock that is being staged prior to shipping for a current order. If there is stock in the warehouse of a make-to-order item, it is very likely that this stock will never be sold (because it is usually unique to one customer and often unique to one order). Any leftover stock for make-to-order items is a problem that must be addressed.

I often observe companies mixing up their finished goods strategies. These companies often accumulate large amounts of obsolete stock of make-to-order items that are never ordered again. Then in the same warehouse, they will run out of stock of other items that customers expect to order off-the-shelf.

It is rare that I find a company where all their products fit within one finished goods strategy. Most businesses have a mix of both strategies. However, as a general rule, businesses that have a standard range of products they market and sell (such as fast-moving consumer goods manufacturers) will tend to keep their range in stock. On the other hand, manufacturers of customized products such as boat builders (or jobbing manufacturers such as sheet metal shops and packaging manufacturers) tend to produce make-to-order products. A key determinant is the customer's expectations of service. For example, if your customer expects next-day delivery but your production process takes 2 weeks, you will probably need to hold stock unless you can find a way to reduce your lead-time to 1 day. On the other hand, if your customer expects a customized product and is prepared to wait 8 weeks (as an example, a new piece of machinery or a structural steel component for a building), you are most likely to make-to-order.

Can You Combine or Eliminate Processes?

Now that we know how much we need to make (our *takt* time), and how we are going to supply our customer (our finished goods strategy), we can turn our focus to the manufacturing process.

The first question we ask is: Are there any processes we can combine or eliminate altogether? The quick answer I always get to this question is: "No, we need all our processes." That cuts off any further possibilities of reducing costs and lead-times. Therefore, I suggest you take a step-by-step approach. Examine each product step in turn and ask the following questions: What would our process look like without this step? Can we achieve the same outcome without this process? Can we incorporate this process within another process? Look critically at inspection steps and work-in-progress (WIP) packaging steps. Often, these are overprocessing and can be eliminated. Some examples we have encountered include the following:

A machining shop was manufacturing a complex part. The part was initially rough-machined from a billet of stainless steel. It was then taken to the metrology department and measured before being returned to a machine for second-stage machining. It was returned to metrology to be measured again. It was then heat-treated (which changed the dimensions) and subjected to a final machining step. After this, the part returned to metrology for a full dimensional analysis on a coordinate-measuring machine (CMM). We established that the checks after rough and secondary machining were repetitive and unnecessary. These steps were eliminated, and the rough and secondary machining operations were combined into a single operation with a quick dimensional check being done on the part between stages while it remained in the machine. This saved days of lead-time and eliminated machine setups.

Another one of our customers was a manufacturer of doors. At the end of assembly, each door was stacked on a specially designed pallet for transport to the dispatch warehouse. The doors were then removed from the pallets and packed in a cardboard box for shipment. After mapping their value stream, the customer realized that with some changes to the layout, they could pack the doors in a box on the assembly line. This process eliminated double-handling the doors on and off the pallets, eliminated the separate dispatch and packing area, and prevented damage to the doors as the box protected them as soon as they were assembled.

How Do We Flow Products between Processes?

Once we have eliminated the unnecessary processes, we next decide how to flow the products from one process to the next. There are three options:

1. Create one-piece flow or a work cell.
2. Control the process with a first-in-first-out (FIFO) lane.
3. Establish a supermarket of parts between processes that is replenished by a pull system or *Kanban* system from the upstream process.

As mentioned previously, experts have written entire books on value stream mapping and how to flow products from one process to another. Consequently, this is a summary. Alternatively, there is real value in seeking the help of an expert such as one of the team members at TXM to coach you through the value stream mapping process.

Creating One-Piece Flow

One-piece flow is truly amazing. For those of us brought up on the concept of economic order quantities and the idea that big batches are efficient, the concept that you should flow products through a series of product steps one at a time is totally counterintuitive. However, once you have seen a one-piece flow cell in action and observed how dramatically it slashes wasted time in a process, you will never want to run a big batch again!

When you examine the processes in your current state map, ask this question: Is there any reason why this process cannot be combined into one-piece flow? If you cannot come up with a good reason, try placing the processes beside each other and flowing the product from one process to another, one at a time. There are a number of reasons we might find why we cannot implement one-piece flow. These include

- One or both processes have long setup times, meaning that one process will be waiting for the other to be set up.
- The processes work at different speeds or have different work content. This means that the fast process will always be waiting for the slow processes, thereby creating a bottleneck.
- The processes are physically separate (perhaps in different buildings).
- The processes operate on different shifts; for example, one process operates on two shifts while the other operates on one shift.

In my experience, in almost every case I have seen, given enough determination, these barriers can be overcome. Setup times can be reduced or even eliminated. Processes can be balanced or a level of machine downtime accepted in the interest of the efficiency of the entire process. Shifts can be balanced, and machinery and people can be relocated to create a cell. If you make the effort, you will eliminate the waste between each step and bring your lead-time closer to your value-added time. Creating one-piece flow also enables you to quickly highlight waste such as waiting time, defects, or breakdowns that might be hidden by inventory buffers. Once you see these hidden barriers to flow, you can eliminate them, and the savings are often dramatic. Here is an example.

One of our customers manufactures heavy truck fuel tanks. Heavy trucks (greater than 10-ton gross vehicle mass) are highly customized, and the fuel tanks are no exception with a huge range and combination of sizes, outlets, brackets, and internal baffles. However, they all go through a common set of processes, and all form a single value stream. Our customer set up a flow cell to build fuel tanks with dedicated punching, rolling, welding, polishing, and testing processes all in line. We helped them install simple systems to replenish components to this line. The customer can now make a finished tank from a blank sheet in less than 2 days and at a cost much lower than competitors still using the old batch-and-queue method. As a result, our customer now dominates their market, and their customers are giving them a wider and wider range of components to manufacture, all of which are being made in cells.

First-In-First-Out

While one-piece flow is the best waste removal tool in the Lean manufacturing armory, sometimes it is just not possible to create a cell. This might be because machines are shared, machines work at different rates, machines have longer changeover times, or machines have fixed batch sizes.

To control the flow between these processes, first-in-first-out (FIFO) is very effective. As a tool in Lean manufacturing, FIFO has a very specific meaning. It is usually a controlled location for WIP where the first job or batch from the upstream process is *always* the first process downstream. Second, the amount of work allowed to queue in a FIFO lane is always limited. When the queue is full, the upstream process must stop to allow the downstream process to catch up. In this way, a FIFO lane ensures that the backlog and lead-time between two processes is tightly controlled. When the FIFO sequence is maintained, you ensure that the lead-time is consistent for all jobs.

Physically, a FIFO lane can take many forms. It can be an area marked on the plant floor with just enough space for the maximum WIP, and an arrow showing the direction of flow. Even better is a gravity roller conveyor where the product is fed by the upstream process and uses gravity to flow down to the next station, in sequence. The length of the conveyor is set to accommodate the maximum amount of WIP.

In some cases, the product is simply too big to move along a FIFO lane and a trolley, or a roller conveyor is not available. In these cases, an alternative is to control the flow of the production information associated with the job. Information such as drawings, bills of materials, and production and quality instructions are usually circulated with the batch. By controlling

Figure 4.2   This worker at Branach (see Chapter 1) receives his production instructions in FIFO sequence, taking the next job from the left-hand end of the "curtain rail" while new jobs are fed in from the right. The length of the rail controls the amount of jobs in the queue.

these in a FIFO sequence, production can be controlled without the need to physically move all products along a FIFO lane. This job sheet FIFO approach is particularly effective for jobbing processes.

There are many more alternative approaches to setting up a FIFO (such as the example in Figure 4.2), but for jobbing and customized products, the FIFO lane can be very effective in controlling the flow and preventing excessive buildup of WIP between workstations, as described in the paragraph above. This, in turn, can lead to dramatic reductions in lead-time and WIP inventory—in our experience, up to 80%.

If FIFO Is Not Possible, Then Pull

If you cannot make FIFO operate successfully, you should consider implementing a pull system or *Kanban* system, where the upstream process only replenishes what the downstream process uses. *Kanban* systems are a large subject on their own, that we cover in more detail later. I also recommend that you read *Making Materials Flow.*[4]

Traditional systems for planning are based on push. That is, we push materials and products through to each process based on the amount of product we expect to manufacture in the future. The problem with this approach is that we cannot exactly predict the future and usually flood the production system with the wrong quantity of materials in the wrong place at the wrong time. I discuss this more in Chapters 8 and 9. While managers tend to view Lean pull systems as complex, they are, in fact, simple and more reliable than a push system. With a pull system, we only order materials from the upstream process or the supplier when we use those materials. The management of materials in a pull system is often described as a supermarket because it operates in a similar way. The shelves in a supermarket are restocked as products are sold. The quantity stocked in each location is determined by the average sales of each item so that stock does not run out during the day. Shelves are replenished at night by replacing stock that has been sold during the just-completed day. This is essentially how a pull system operates.

The advantage of this approach is that the downstream process only receives the parts it needs. It also is less prone to errors as replenishment is based on actual usage rather than a potentially inaccurate forecast. The disadvantage of setting up a supermarket-type pull system is that it builds in a level of inventory between processes and, as we know, inventory is waste. Therefore, we should always try to use one-piece flow or a FIFO lane before considering a pull system.

Controlling the Release of Work to Production

In typical production processes, we often try to plan each process. We take customer orders and develop a master plan. From this master plan we calculate a plan for each production step and release these plans to each manufacturing department. I liken this approach to the conductor of an orchestra taking the music score and breaking it into the various departments—strings, woodwind, percussion, brass—and then handing these scores to the departmental conductors. These departmental conductors then start conducting the music for their departments. At the end of the piece, they report back to the head conductor on how it sounded. I have no doubt that individually the sound produced by the strings department and the woodwind department would be great. However, I am equally sure that the sound produced by an entire orchestra managed this way would be truly terrible. *Therefore, just as an orchestra needs a single conductor, a production process needs a pacemaker.* This is usually the process that is farthest upstream of any FIFO lane or production cell, but downstream of any pull or *Kanban* system. This is because a *Kanban* system will only replenish what the downstream process uses and is therefore responding to usage rather than to customer orders. Customer orders should be sent to this pacemaker process, and the pacemaker process needs to determine the sequence and rate at which that work is released. I discuss in more detail how we release work to the factory via the *pacemaker process* described in Chapter 8.

Some Tips on Value Stream Mapping

Based on experience, there are some simple rules to follow that will help avoid some of the common pitfalls of value stream mapping:

- Always map the entire flow, from receipt of materials to dispatch of finished goods. I constantly hear people talk about mapping a "department." This misses the whole point. Value stream mapping is about breaking down organizational silos and aligning your structure to your customer. Mapping a single department tends to reinforce your organizational silos.
- Do one value stream at a time. If you do it properly, you will find that two or three core value streams will represent most of what you do. Focus on these and get them right, rather than trying to map everything at once. Only attempt two value streams at once if the products are closely related and share a lot of common routings and equipment.
- Always complete the future state and an action plan before moving on to the next value stream. Just doing a current state map does not take your business anywhere. Likewise, doing a future state map without developing a detailed plan about how you will implement it means that it is unlikely there will be any action taken to implement the future state.
- Get professional help. Value stream mapping is a complex technique to implement well and requires someone with a deep Lean knowledge and excellent facilitation skills to lead the process. I learned value stream mapping the hard way—through trial and error with a copy of *Learning to See* sitting on my lap. You can take this approach but,

quite frankly, my experience taught me that "doing it yourself" will take longer, cost more, and give a much poorer outcome than biting the bullet and hiring a good Lean consultant.

Pulling It All Together

This chapter was intended as a very quick introduction to value stream mapping, and we recommend that you read some of the texts we suggest or engage a specialist such as TXM to coach you through the use of this powerful tool. However, understanding your current state and developing a plan for your future state is the first step in developing your production process. We coach customers to develop an A3 plan to implement their value stream map. This is a simple one-page plan that (for a value stream map) summarizes the current state, the future state, the action plan to get from the current state to the future state, and the measurable improvements we expect the future state to deliver. Figure 4.3 shows a completed future state map for the process presented in Figure 4.1.

Key Points in Chapter 4

- Improving manufacturing processes starts with improving product flow, and the best way to understand and improve product flow is with a value stream map.
- Before starting your value stream map, you need to define your product families. These are the broad flows of product through your business. They are usually defined as groups of products that follow the same or similar routings.
- Make sure you always choose your most important product family as the target of your first value stream. It is easier to rearrange the flow of lesser products around an important product than the other way around.
- Your *takt* time is the average rate at which you sell your products (not make them). When you level your rate of production to match your *takt* time, you minimize the seven wastes in your processes.
- For each of your products, you need to decide up-front whether they are make-to-stock or make-to-order. Make-to-stock products should normally be in stock, whereas you should only have stock of make-to-order products if they are for a current open order.

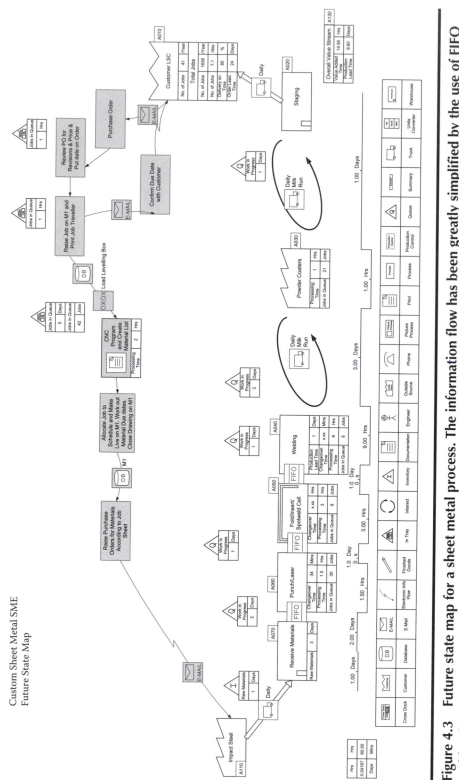

Custom Sheet Metal SME
Future State Map

Figure 4.3 Future state map for a sheet metal process. The information flow has been greatly simplified by the use of FIFO and leveling of order release. A daily "milk run" takes products back and forth to the powder coating subcontractor.

- In developing your revised production flow, you need to first try and create one-piece flow, where products flow one at a time from one process to the next. If one-piece flow is not possible, then a FIFO lane is a very simple and effective way to control the flow between processes. Finally, if it is not possible to flow the product at all, you should try a *Kanban* system or pull system.
- You should only release new production orders at one point in the process. All flow, upstream or downstream from this point, can then be controlled by FIFO lanes (downstream) or *Kanban* pull systems (upstream).

References

1. Womack, J.P. and Jones, D.T. 2003. *Lean Thinking.* New York: Free Press.
2. Rother, M. and Shook, J. 2003. *Learning to See: Value-Stream Mapping to Create Value and Eliminate Muda.* Brookline, MA: Lean Enterprise Institute.
3. Duggan, K.J. 2002. *Creating Mixed Model Value Streams: Practical Lean Techniques for Building to Demand,* New York: Productivity Press.
4. Harris, R., Harris, C., and Wilson, E. 2003. *Making Materials Flow: A Lean Material-Handling Guide for Operations, Production-Control, and Engineering Professionals.* Cambridge, MA: Lean Enterprise Institute.

Chapter 5

Getting the Right Layout and Equipment

What You Will Learn in This Chapter

- How to develop a more productive plant layout for your factory
- Why it is important to put your customer first in developing a plant layout
- How to decide whether to purchase new machinery or automation for your plant to give you the best return on investment

Don't Start Your Future Factory Planning at a Machinery Exhibition

In our experience, many manufacturers start their future factory planning at a machinery exhibition by seeing a piece of new equipment and visualizing the benefits that that machine can deliver to their businesses. Machinery exhibitions are very impressive. All kinds of new high-technology equipment are on display in showroom condition. The machines are usually set up by technical specialists to run perfectly at their peak performance.

Likewise, it is exciting to tour vacant factories or industrial estates with an estate agent and visualize your business operating in a gleaming new building.

Before you reach for your checkbook or call your banker, you should know that selecting new equipment and a new building are among the last things you need to determine when deciding the future of your factory.

Every year, our company, TXM, has an exhibit at a major plant and machinery exhibition. Our logic has always been that for a fraction of the cost of a new machine or a new piece of software, a customer can achieve a much greater savings or capacity increase by improving what it has using Lean manufacturing.

You will find businesses where the owner has located a great piece of equipment or a grandiose factory building, purchased it, and then successfully found work to fill its capacity. However, I suspect that for every one of these so-called success stories, you will also find several examples of companies that have gone bankrupt by putting the hardware and building selections first.

Planning Your New Factory: Put the Customer First

Before you think about machinery or building, the starting point for your new factory is your customer. You need to begin the process of determining your factory's future by forgetting about buildings and machines, and start focusing on what the customer wants. You need to build a forecast of what you think will sell. The forecast needed for planning your investments will most likely be a 5-year timeline, as major investments usually pay back over years, not months. Unless your business is highly seasonal, it is probably adequate to make this forecast in increments of 1 year, rather than months, and at the highest product level (value streams). If your business is highly seasonal, then your investment planning needs to provide production capacity for your peak monthly or quarterly demand each year.

When developing your forecast, it is important that you clearly think through and document assumptions. For example, if you are anticipating 20% sales growth, document your assumption showing where the growth will come from, and explain why you selected 20% growth, not 10% or 30%.

You may also need to make assumptions on product mix. These assumptions will be important for you to refer to so the people who are financing your project understand the basis for your decision making (whether that be private investment money or money allocated by corporate head office and shareholders in the case of a division of a large public company).

From Chapter 4 you know how to calculate *takt* time as the rate of customer demand. You now need to calculate *takt* time over your 5-year investment forecast period.

Table 5.1   Example of a 5-Year High-Level Forecast for a Factory

Value Stream	Year 0 (current)	Year 1	Year 2	Year 3	Year 4	Year 5
Motor Homes						
Growth%	—	10%	10%	10%	5%	5%
Motor Homes (units)	200	220	242	266	278	292
Motor Homes *Takt* Time (hrs.)	9.0	8.2	7.4	6.8	6.5	6.2
Caravans Growth%	—	20%	20%	10%	10%	5%
Caravans (units)	500	600	720	790	860	900
Caravan *Takt* Time (hrs.)	3.6	3.0	2.5	2.3	2.1	2.0

To understand this, it helps to think about a practical example. Let's imagine a factory building caravans and motor homes on a single 8-hour shift (figuring 1,800 working hours per year). For this factory, the 5-year forecast will appear as a table similar to Table 5.1.

From Table 5.1 you can see how on one shift, the *takt* time for motor homes decreases over the 5-year period from 9.0 hours to 6.2 hours, and the *takt* time for a caravan decreases from 3.6 hours to 2.0 hours. In practical terms, this means that on one shift the factory would need to increase output from around one motor home and two caravans per day up to 1.5 motor homes and four caravans per day. If this rate was not achievable (because the production cycle time was too long), then the business would have the choice of either

- Increasing the planned working hours by adding additional shifts, or
- Reducing the cycle time to below the *takt* time by changing the production process.

It is likely that your plan will highlight a number of improvements that need to be made over the 5-year period to meet the growing demand for products. We explain this process later in this chapter.

Converting the Value Stream to a Layout

Chapter 4 explained how to develop a value stream map and determine your product flow. This is now the next step in developing your new factory.

Assemble a team that represents your whole end-to-end process—from raw materials through to finished goods. If you are working on the plant layout, this team needs to include employees who actually work on the factory floor and who understand the process in a practical sense. This means front-line team leaders or senior workers as well as key functional managers. Usually, a value stream mapping and plant layout development team will involve between four and twelve employees.

It is better to avoid letting the team become too large. For a big factory, you might do this at two levels, with a more senior team looking at the overall value stream and a shop-floor team focusing on the design of individual production work cells.

TIP: Even if you are planning on upgrading just part of your factory (e.g., the chassis welding in the caravan and motor home example), it pays to map the whole end-to-end value stream from receiving materials to dispatching finished goods. This enables you to see how your plant upgrade impacts the whole value stream. We often see companies invest in localized plant upgrades that do not deliver the expected benefits because of a failure to account for the impact on upstream and downstream processes.

You need to develop a future state map for your key value streams. Start by completing the future state for Year 1 (the beginning of the forecast period). This will determine the amount of inventory required at each point in the process, how production will flow through the factory, and the required number of operating hours for key machines and production cells.

Analyzing Capacity

Using *takt* time as a yardstick, determining if you have enough capacity is relatively simple. A production capacity chart such as Figure 5.1 can give you a clear view of your capacity across the value stream compared to *takt* time.

In the example shown in Figure 5.1, you can clearly see that a number of processes, notably painting, exceed the *takt* time. To meet customer demand, all processes must be able to complete one unit of production in less than *takt* time. Therefore, the team needs to determine ways to ensure that each process can be completed under *takt* time. These actions might include

- Running extra shifts (which will extend the *takt* time)
- Spreading the tasks over more workers (you can see how each process includes multiple tasks)

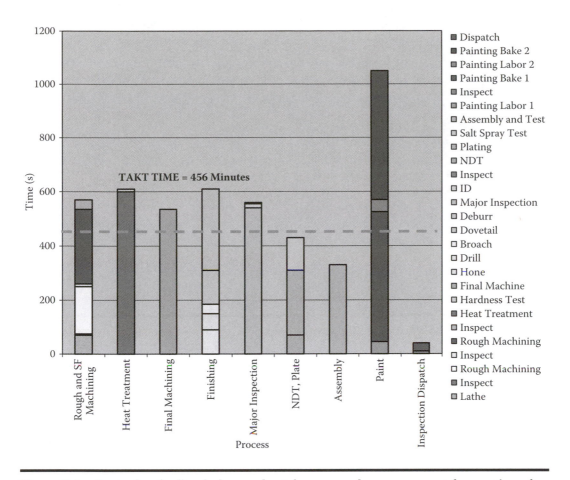

Figure 5.1 Example of a line balance chart for a complex component for an aircraft.

- Combining tasks in different ways to level the workload
- Adding additional machines

In the example begun above, a series of improvements was made, including elimination of some inspection and machining tasks and splitting the painting task into two steps (requiring an additional worker). These processes enabled the product to be completed within *takt* time, although further work could be done to balance the workload more across all the process steps. Figure 5.2 shows the result of these changes.

From this process you will have an initial list of actions and perhaps some investments and recruiting decisions needed for Year 1. You should repeat this exercise for each year of your 5-year forecast. As your business grows, the *takt* time will become shorter, and you will need to make further adjustments to ensure that the process can be completed within *takt* time.

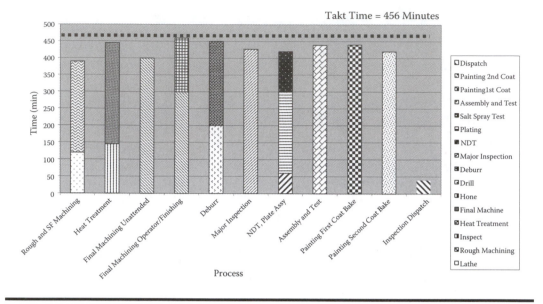

Figure 5.2 Line balance chart for component process after process adjustments to meet *takt* time.

For example, from Table 5.1, the paint baking process is at capacity at one product per day. To increase capacity and reduce *takt* time, it will be necessary to increase baking throughput. This means either reducing the baking time (which is not possible in this case because the paint system is often specified by the customer and subject to long approval cycles), or increasing the baking capacity by buying more baking ovens. Therefore, we can expect that paint baking capacity will be an investment needed in Year 2 for this business if it is to grow beyond one product per day.

Once you have completed your value stream and your capacity analysis for the 5-year forecast, you will have a clear idea of

- What equipment you will need and when you will need it
- What raw material and finished goods inventory you will need to hold
- How product will flow through your factory and what work-in-progress (WIP) storage you will need
- How many employees you will need at each step of your process and what shifts they will need to work
- How requirements for equipment, materials, and people will increase over the 5-year forecast period

This is essentially all the information required to start developing your plant layout.

Developing the Layout

People are visual creatures; we understand best what we can see. It is important to realize that not everyone can read a two-dimensional drawing. Therefore, we find that the layout needs to be a tactile process where everyone gets to touch the elements of the layout and move them around.

Start by measuring the outer dimensions of all your equipment, including equipment you are likely to purchase. Find a large smooth table, ideally so large that people can barely reach the center. Obtain information on critical dimensions such as pallet sizes, forklift aisle widths, separation of machinery, width of pedestrian aisles and access ways, etc.

Then the fun begins. You need to create a scale cut from card (or even better, a three-dimensional shape made from balsa or polystyrene foam) for each piece of machinery and other fixed items such as pallets, storage racks, and material handling equipment such as conveyors. I typically use a 1:50 scale. However, for a small layout, use a bigger scale (e.g., 1:20) and try to avoid going any smaller than 1:100 as then everything becomes too small. Try to be as accurate as you can rather than, for example, just cutting out everything as rectangles or deliberately making shapes oversized.

Once you have cut out the shapes, assemble your team around the big table you have chosen. Make sure your future state value stream map is up on the wall in the room and start your layout. Follow your value stream map, starting at the customer (usually shipping), and work backward to follow the process to the starting stage. Make sure you allow space for machines and only the inventory you have planned in your future state map. Ensure that you allow sufficient, but not excessive, space between pieces of equipment. It pays to measure actual distances between each piece of your current equipment. Either that or consult manufacturers' recommendations, as I find that people usually overestimate how much space they need between machines. Allow for material handling flows and pedestrian access (refer to *Making Materials Flow*[1] for help on how to design efficient material handling flows). At this stage, if you are laying out an existing building, *do not* try to fit the layout to your building; just focus on designing the perfect flow for your process.

Design the flow to minimize the use of forklifts and cranes. Forklifts are great space wasters (forklift aisles can be between 3 and 5 meters wide) and are a major safety challenge in any factory. Therefore, try to place workstations so that one feeds the other, and so that product can be moved by hand from one stage to the next. Likewise, cranes bring their own safety issues but are also a source of waste because they inevitably create waiting time as workers complete tasks and must wait for the use of the crane to move their products forward. I have seen some great innovations with the use of hovercraft-style skids, conveyors, or trolleys to enable moving heavy product along the line without the use of cranes.

Base your flow on existing technology. While I refer to a perfect flow, that does not mean solving everything with automated solutions you do not already have and may not even exist; or if they exist may be unaffordable. It is better to design the layout for your current materials handling equipment and materials, and then selectively look at where automation may improve this further, and how that automation investment can be justified. We often see companies overautomate new plants. This can greatly increase the capital cost and complexity of a new plant and heighten the implementation risk on start-up. Had those automation plans been assessed individually, they often would not be financially justified.

Start with the main product flow (your main value stream) and then build secondary value streams and subassembly production around it. In that way, you ensure that the most important flows are also the most optimal.

Eventually you will have a conceptual layout on your table such as the one in Figure 5.3 for a corrugated box factory. We use double-sided tape or Blu Tack (reusable putty) to stick the shapes to the table. Next, take a

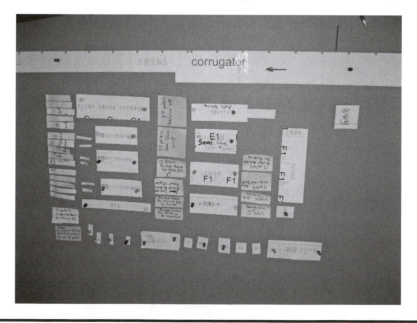

Figure 5.3 Conceptual layout for a corrugated box factory with the corrugators feeding board from left to right and then the processing steps flowing right to left.

quality photograph of this layout so that you always have on file the original concept you were trying to achieve. You can project this on the wall in the meeting room when you go to the next stage. Even better, if you have duplicated all your scale shapes, you can use the second set of shapes for the following stage of layout development.

If you are developing a layout for a new plant, this conceptual layout can be the basis for your new building design. However, more often than not, you will develop a layout for an existing building. Therefore, the next step is to fit this layout to your actual building. For this, you need a layout drawing on the same scale as you have made for the cutouts of your machinery and inventory. It is important that the layout drawing shows key details in the building, such as structural columns, doors, internal walls, and other key features.

You then start the process of transferring the conceptual layout to the real building. Once again, start at the loading dock and move backward through the process to receiving. Try to hold as much as possible to the original concept you established. Where you do have to make compromises to your concepts, note these (perhaps on a whiteboard in the meeting room) and discuss their impact and whether they can be overcome (e.g., by building modifications). You will likely be surprised how easy this is. We find that developing a conceptual layout first often leads businesses to discover that they need less space than at first expected.

At the end of this process, you will have a layout fitted to your building and list of key decisions about building changes (such as removal of a wall or creation of doors) that might be necessary to accommodate it. Figure 5.4 shows an example of this final "fitted" layout for the corrugated box factory layout shown in Figure 5.3.

For a much more detailed description of the process of designing your plant and your workstations to achieve level production, I recommend *Creating Continuous Flow* by Rother and Harris.[*]

The final step then is to get a CAD (computer-aided design) draftsperson to draw up your layout. This makes a permanent record of your layout (cutouts of machinery tend to fall off, get lost, or be moved), and can be used to design the layout of mechanical and electrical services to the machines. The CAD layout is also likely to reveal some practical issues with the layout (e.g., equipment in front of fire-hose reels, excessive or unrealistic

---

[*] Rother, M. and Harris, R. 2001. *Creating Continuous Flow: An Action Guide for Managers, Engineers and Production Associates*. Cambridge, MA: Lean Enterprise Institute.

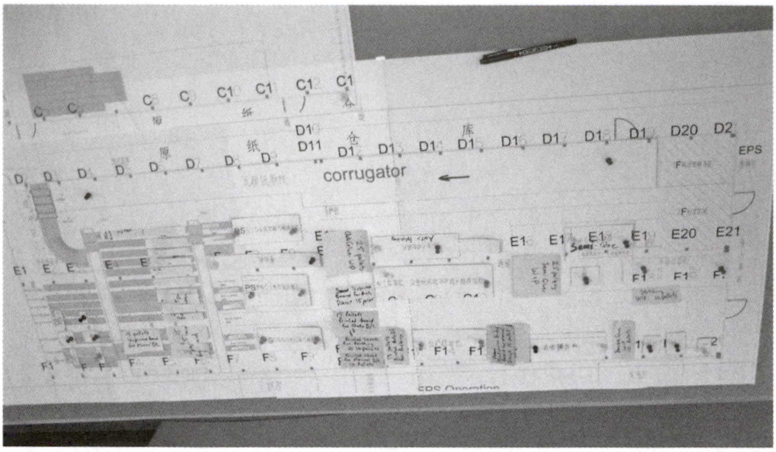

Figure 5.4 Corrugated box layout fitted to the building. In this case, the required changes to the conceptual layout were minor. However, the new layout achieved a 40% space saving by combining activities that were previously spread over two factories into one.

spacing, etc.). It is therefore a smart idea for the team to perform a final review of the CAD layout with the draftsperson in the room so that changes to the layout caused by these practical issues do not undermine the original concept of the layout.

The next task is to develop a budget for the implementation of the layout. Typical major costs include

- Building modifications and repairs in the case of an existing building
- Provision of electricity, water, power (and perhaps gas) to the equipment and workstations
- Construction of storage racks for materials
- Disconnection or reconnection of equipment (for complex equipment, external expertise from the machinery vendor may be needed for relocation)
- Provision of cranes and equipment for the physical relocation of the equipment

Develop a detailed budget for your relocation and then I highly recommend that you (or your accountant) complete a rigorous financial analysis of your investment, usually a profit-and-loss and balance sheet forecast and discounted cash flow analysis. I do not intend to write a treatise on investment analysis here, so I suggest you get professional advice on this one. It is telling that in every major corporation I have worked, full financial analysis was required for every investment, and great rigor was applied to ensure that every capital investment gave a return that exceeded the corporation's minimum return-on-investment target. Too often, I see the owners of small and medium-sized enterprises (SMEs) focused on the cost and not the benefits of new investment. They lock themselves into years and years of poor returns by purchasing assets that would never have passed a financial cost-benefit analysis. However, if the financial analysis stacks up, then you have designed a fantastic new facility to support the growth of your business for the next 5 years and beyond.

Plant Layout Redesign Case Study: Sykes Racing

Background: The Need for Change at Sykes Racing

When you walk into a customer's manufacturing facilities and see a wall of photographs displaying Olympic gold medals won using the company's products, you know you are visiting a special place. This was the circumstance 5 years ago when TXM first visited Sykes Racing in Geelong, Australia (www. sykes.com.au). Over the past 30 years, 75% of Australia's Olympic and World Championship rowing medals have been won in Sykes boats. Many members of the management team have rowed at the highest level, and this determination to succeed was one of the key factors enabling Sykes to pull off one of the most radical Lean transformations of any TXM customer.

Prior to the global financial crisis of 2008, Sykes Racing was spread across several small factory buildings on the side of a hill next to the Barwon River. This picturesque location was ideal for getting out for a row at lunchtime, but far from ideal for manufacturing.

Sykes boats had transformed from wood to sophisticated carbon fiber composites many years before, but the manufacturing mind-set remained largely unchanged. A traditional craft approach was used in which one person built the boat from start to finish. Almost every boat needed some reworking at final inspection, where the most skilled craftsmen looked over the boat from top to bottom. The result of this approach was highly variable output and little control over backlog (Figures 5.5 and 5.6 show the Sykes Racing factory prior to the Lean Transformation project). At the time of starting the project, Sykes had a backlog of 6 months and was coming under pressure from imported Chinese boats.

Figure 5.5   The boat building area at the old Sykes factory was very congested.

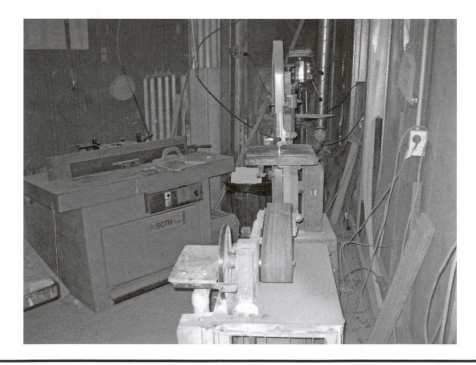

Figure 5.6   There was a lack of organization at the old Sykes site.

The TXM Approach

TXM coached the Sykes team to develop a value stream map. However, the rubber really hit the road when Sykes applied the TXM plant layout process to the long, thin rowing boats. The result was an "S"-shaped flow layout that enabled the business to potentially double output, but locked it into moving from "one man builds the boat" to one-piece flow and standard work. The layout change meant moving the boat through a series of manufacturing process steps at a rate of one boat per day. A small FIFO (first-in-first-out) lane was set up between the laminating and fit-out process; but apart from that, the boats needed to move every day to keep the process flowing.

Sykes Racing performed standard work analysis of every process step in order to level the amount of work at each workstation. This was complicated by the fact that every boat is different, and the standard work had to allow for this. Subsequently, Sykes used what the TXM team calls *Fuzzy Standard* work, where work elements are measured in minutes and some variation in cycle times from job to job is allowed.

Adding complexity were the anodized aluminum riggers used to mount the oars on the boats. These parts were produced in parallel to the boat manufacturing through an entirely different process. Delays to riggers were a frequent cause of holdups in finishing boats. Sykes developed an improved flow in their metal shop to ensure that riggers were delivered early and were on hand when the boat reached the end of the line.

Apart from ensuring the flow, the standard work process led to significant productivity benefits, as differences in the time taken to complete tasks were highlighted and all workers trained to follow the best method. After some initial teething issues, this standardization of method has led to further improvement in Sykes' already high-quality standards.

The Final Step

Once the standard work was under way, the final stage shifted the focus back to reinforcing the Lean foundations. This most notably included structured problem solving, 5S, and Lean daily management where team leaders coach their teams through short daily stand-up meetings. This daily focus ensured that Sykes stabilized its processes and continued to improve.

The results have been outstanding. As well as having a spotless factory that now leads the world in productivity and quality, Sykes has reduced its order backlog from 6 months to 6 weeks, along with increased output, increased productivity, and reduced rework.

As Jeff Lawrence of Sykes says, "The empowerment, knowledge, opportunity, and satisfaction that has come to the shop floor has been nothing short of spectacular in terms of the commitment to improvement and the participation in the journey. Our most cynical people have become our main Lean advocates."

An example of the success of the project was a recent order of 20 identical boats, which were produced more than 60 hours faster than the company had been able to achieve 2 years prior. The quickest one of the batch was produced more than 120 hours faster than the company was achieving 10 years ago.

"The whole process," Jeff said, "has really opened everyone's mind to the opportunities to make further improvement across our range." Figure 5.7 shows the Sykes Racing plant today.*

Figure 5.7　Sykes Racing "flow production" layout today. Boats "flow" through the plant at a *takt* time of 1 day.

---

* To view an interview with Jeff Lawrence from Sykes Racing, go to http://txm.com.au/video/txm-lean-case-study-video-sykes-racing-lean-for-customised-manufacturing

Key Points in Chapter 5

The largest and most important investment of your business will be a new factory and new equipment. Therefore, it is critical to get this right. The steps in this process are

■ Design your new factory *before* you go to a machinery exhibition and select new equipment.

■ In designing your plant, start with the customer. What key products do you expect to sell over the next 5 years? Develop a high-level annual forecast and document your assumptions.

■ Map your key value streams as described in Chapter 4 and develop your future state and *takt* time for each year of the 5-year forecast period to determine future requirements for machinery, people, and inventory.

■ Cut out all your machine templates and materials to scale and assemble a team of all the key leaders in your factory to develop the layout.

■ First, devise an "ideal layout" without the constraint of trying to fit it to a building. Just focus on devising the best layout possible.

■ Keep it simple and avoid bold plans for automation, particularly if proven automation solutions are not available.

■ Automation investments should be justified individually and not just rolled into the overall project cost.

■ If you have already chosen a building, the next step is to fit the "ideal layout" to your building. You will find this surprisingly easy. Changes will be required, so take steps to ensure that you document deviations from your ideal layout to keep in step with your original layout concept.

■ Get a CAD draftsperson to draw your layout plan, but again make sure that any changes made do not compromise your original ideal concept.

■ Construct a budget and perform a proper cost-benefit financial analysis for your new factory to ensure an adequate financial return.

Chapter 6

Developing an Organizational Structure and the Leadership to Sustain It

What You Will Learn in This Chapter

- The importance of aligning your organizational structure with your value streams
- How to organize your shop-floor teams, and the importance and role of your front-line leaders
- Tips on how to recruit the right people for your business
- Why firing your managers and hiring new ones is usually not the best way to improve your business performance

Getting Started at Developing an Organizational Structure

I am sure that I will receive a lot of criticism for not putting employees first in the leading chapter of this book. I accept that, but before you can work out who you need on your team and how to structure your organization, you first need to know what you are making and how you are making it. If you have taken my advice in the first 5 chapters of this book, you will have faced and conquered that hurdle. You can calculate the labor-hours required and determine how many workers and how many shifts you need to fulfill your strategic objectives.

When your business is very small (fewer than 10 employees), you will typically have two organizational levels: (1) the manager or owner and

(2) the workers. As the business grows, most small and medium-sized enterprises (SMEs) introduce a layer of first-line supervisors to organize, supervise, and support production workers. These front-line leaders are usually selected from among the most experienced and capable workers. Finally, once the business reaches 30 employees, middle managers are introduced, such as a production or operations manager, warehouse manager, and possibly initial staff roles such as quality manager, purchasing manager, and a planning manager. This is the point where you will need to start injecting some "Lean Thinking" into your organizational structure if you are to control the growth of your overheads and grow profitably.

A Value Stream Structure for Middle Management

It is our belief at TXM that a value stream is the best place to start building your organizational structure. This is because it creates a direct alignment between the needs of your customers (what you need to make), your processes (how you make it), and the roles of all employees in your organization.

In most businesses, the natural tendency will be to structure the team along process lines. That translates into employing a machine shop manager, a welding shop manager, and an assembly manager. In the paint industry, you might have managers responsible for dispersion, mixing, quality control, color matching, and filling; and in a packaging factory, a materials supervisor, a print supervisor, a die cutting supervisor, and a finishing supervisor.

There is some logic in this approach, and it is perhaps unavoidable for front-line roles, because the skills required for coaching a team in a machine shop are quite different from those required in an assembly cell, due to the different technologies involved. However, as you move up the organization, you need to challenge this process-centric organization and try to organize your factory as your customer sees it—in value streams.

The problem with the process-centric structure is that once you put someone in charge of a process department, you tend to align their performance measures and their focus to that one specific department. The manager of that department has the responsibility of optimizing operations in that one specific area only. This often puts the manager in conflict with the needs of the overall value stream. For example, the supervisor of a packaging printing department is likely to be measured on the number of sheets or meters of output from printing. The overall output from the value stream and the fact that he might be flooding the finishing area with work-in-progress (WIP) is not his concern. He will also be reluctant to run shorter runs or slow production to match demand because it may reduce the output of the printers and make his personal performance metrics look bad, *even if the additional printer output is not needed.* Introducing one-piece flow becomes difficult or almost impossible as it involves bringing assets from multiple departments together into one cell, *which is in the interest of none of the individual functional departments.* It is much better to start with a value stream and appoint a leader for each value stream, cutting across the process boundaries.

One medium-sized TXM customer grows and processes vegetables. The process typically involves sowing, growing, harvesting, processing, and packaging. Each of these process steps is quite different, and it is typical for this kind of business to be structured along product lines with managers for each department. In particular, the farming activities and processing activities usually have separate reporting lines. However, we were surprised to find that our customer was structured along product lines with a manager responsible for the end-to-end production of a crop or group of crops. The general manager we worked with was in charge of carrots and onions. He had responsibility for the entire process, from selecting and planting the seed to distributing the finished packaged product. This value stream structure enables the general manager to see all issues in the supply chain and ensure that each step of the process focuses on delivering what is needed for the end customer.

Another example involves a major sheet metal company. This business includes all the usual processes involved in sheet metal: cutting, folding, stamping, welding, painting, and assembly. Again, it is typical for supervisors to be appointed to each of these areas and to be measured on process rather than value stream performance. In this case, the customer adopted a hybrid model. The most important value streams, such as the manufacture of truck fuel tanks, are treated as separate production cells with dedicated assets and a dedicated manager. This makes this cell a business within a business and ensures close alignment of every step to the overall needs of the customer. This business also produces a wide range of custom products that do not justify a cell. For these, a process-focused manager is responsible for a wide range of less-important products.

Developing Front-Line Teams

There is a lot of research about the span of control and the corresponding size of teams. In our experience, the optimum size for a production team is around seven to twelve employees (including the team leader or supervisor). The team leader is likely to spend most of his time coaching and supporting the team and ensuring they have the resources to meet their *takt* time. The team leader steps in and works on the line when a team member is absent or in training. However, the main focus of the team leader should generally be on supporting the team rather than doing the work. As a result, he is not directly creating value for the customer and therefore is not considered "productive." Reducing team size to below seven to twelve members may therefore lead to higher production costs.

On the other hand, we see a lot of organizations that try and run much bigger teams, up to 30 or 40 workers per team leader (or supervisor). This might be seen as keeping overhead costs low but it is usually a false economy. The team leader does not have time to provide the support and coaching needed to support 30 to 40 workers. Waste is created when individual workers

- Make mistakes due to inadequate training and supervision
- Have to wait for materials, equipment, or production instructions
- Wait again when the line experiences problems that are unresolved and occur again and again because there is no time for effective problem solving

A TXM customer operated a medium-sized factory with around 150 front-line employees engaged in the assembly of highly complex scientific instruments. The factory was structured around five large teams of 30 workers each. TXM observed that team leaders spent their days reacting to the most urgent and pressing issues of the moment: for example, a material shortage, a quality fault, or a product trial. Large amounts of worker time were lost when a problem was encountered, and the worker had to wait while the team leader worked through his other problems and made time to address the worker's issues. Often, the workers left their workstations to seek assistance from engineers or other staff members they thought could help them. This often caused entire production lines to shut down. Many such problems were concealed by a large WIP inventory.

TXM helped this customer redesign its largest line, eliminating WIP buffers and creating one-piece flows. We added additional team leaders so that instead of one team of 30 workers, the revised line was composed of four teams of six to ten workers working on a main assembly line team and three subassembly cell teams. This meant that four workers were taken off their direct-labor jobs and made team leaders. Productivity improved dramatically. The flow line reduced lead-time of 2 weeks to around 2 to 3 days, and improvements developed with the teams reduced labor-hours per unit by 40%, including the hours of the additional team leaders.

What's in a Name? Team Leader or Supervisor?

In the preceding paragraphs, I referred to the front-line lead person as a team leader. In reality, employees in these roles may have different names, including cell leader, shift leader, leading hand, foreperson, or supervisor. In small companies, the front-line leader may be even called the production manager. In our experience, titles do not matter. We are talking about the person whom the front-line worker reports to directly. That said, in some cases we have found that the title of "team leader" can be problematic because there have been frequent misunderstandings and interpretations about the definition of teamwork and autonomous work teams. Employees and managers may have preconceived ideas about what a team leader is, how he or she should be selected, and what specifically the team leader does. If this is the case, I suggest that you do not use the term "team leader."

In a factory I once managed, the term "foreman" was viewed very negatively as that person was seen as a desk-bound sergeant major, barking orders at workers. On the other hand, a past experiment with worker-elected team leaders had been spectacularly unsuccessful. Therefore, we settled on the title "shift leaders." This avoided the negative connotations of the other titles and enabled us to structure the roles in the way we considered best.

We expect that by establishing front-line leaders or team leaders along with a value stream structure for middle management, our organizational structure might look like the example shown in Figure 6.1.

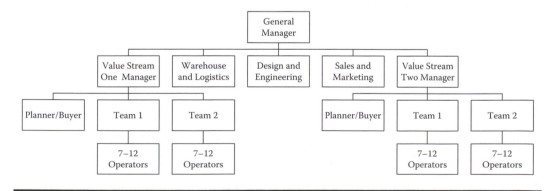

Figure 6.1   Sample organizational structure for a medium-sized manufacturer employing approximately 80 people.

Recruiting the Right People

One of the most important skills in business is the ability to attract and select good people. During my time as a production manager, I decided that it was my single most important decision. One thing I learned: Recruitment is something that should be approached with care and not rushed. Some of my personal do's and don'ts of recruitment areas follow:

■ The first priority is *always* to recruit the right person. If you cannot find the right person, you are better off not recruiting anybody. *Do not rush to fill a role because, inevitably, it will cost you more time and money to fix the problem of recruiting the wrong person.*

■ *Always* advertise job openings internally. A qualified internal person will have a greater probability of success than somebody hired from outside the company. Often, managers believe that the "grass is greener" elsewhere, and they recruit externally without properly considering internal candidates. Failure to provide internal candidates with opportunities for advancement increases the cost of recruitment as well as triggering additional turnover because capable employees become frustrated at being passed over for promotion and leave the company.

■ Don't limit your job search to candidates with (your) industry experience, nor their years of experience. If, for example, you are searching for a supervisor with machining background, you limit the pool of available candidates if you insist on a minimum of 10 years managing a machining shop. While you may not want a lawyer or a bank manager to manage a machine shop, you will find that capable job candidates in other lines of work with an understanding of manufacturing, supplemented by organizational and leadership skills, have the capability of quickly learning your process.

■ Always interview at least three qualified candidates for a role, even if you think you know whom you want for the job. The interviews will help you clarify the qualities and level of experience you need from a successful candidate and give you a clear idea of the kind of candidates on the market.

■ Make sure candidates are interviewed by at least two different managers. You will receive different perspectives about the candidates while also providing candidates with different perspectives about your company.

■ Interviews are about candidates; therefore, make sure they do most of the talking. Typically, candidates should do around 70% of the talking. Use open-ended questions to make sure they have the opportunity to answer questions and respond fully. For example, do not ask, "Did you work for XYZ Company for 5 years?" Instead, say, "Tell me about your accomplishments at XYZ Company."

■ *Always* be honest about the job and your company. Misleading job candidates is foolish because they will find out the truth as soon as they join your company. That is a good way to turn a positive employee into a negative employee, and that is something you do not want to do.

■ Make sure you check references before you recruit anyone. Referees will almost always yield something interesting about the candidate, and this can help you choose the right person and also help you understand better the person you ultimately recruit.

■ Make sure that the employment contract for the person you select includes a trial or probationary period, where you can terminate the new hire if he or she shows signs of being an unproductive employee or troublemaker. Even in the most careful and thorough recruitment processes, mistakes can occur.

■ If you do make a mistake and the person you recruit does not work out, act quickly. The longer you wait, the harder it will be to resolve the issue when the new person does not fit your business.

Developing People: You Cannot Recruit Your Way to Success

As you can well imagine, recruitment is a difficult process. Some managers, particularly in SMEs, think that the answer to business problems is simply to recruit the best people and actively squeeze out employees who do not perform. Sadly in our experience, this approach is frequently a root cause of business failure rather than success. Allow me to explain.

In any business, the effectiveness of its leaders varies. The effectiveness of a leader depends on innate ability, how the leader is perceived by his peers and superiors (which can often be self-fulfilling), the level of training and support provided, the design of the role itself, and transitory factors such as personal issues and short-term business issues. By definition, the average business leader will be of average ability. This is simple statistics. No business sets out to recruit below-average leaders, and few are successful in always finding the upper quartile. Chances are that the team of managers you have is average. It is equally likely that the candidate you recruit after you terminate your last average manager will also be average—which alone should give you pause. If you're not improving the caliber of the terminated employee with a new hire, then why are you terminating the manager?

By terminating one leader and recruiting another, you are exposing your business to considerable cost and risk. First, the recruitment process will typically take 3 months, and a further 3 to 6 months is usually required before the new manager is fully established and able to contribute substantially to improved performance. It is likely too that the new manager will shift the focus of his area of responsibility, meaning that the previous manager's initiatives and improvements will be lost or fail to reach fruition, even when they may have ultimately proved beneficial to the business. We very frequently see this with Lean manufacturing initiatives, which often fall down after a change in leadership, leading to the removal of many of the improvements previously made, This can aggravate cynicism and apathy among surviving team members. This is why W. Edwards Deming highlighted management mobility as one of his *Seven Deadly Diseases*.[1] Finally, even with the most rigorous selection processes, there is a high risk that the new leaders will not be any more effective than the previous leaders.

So what is the alternative? If business performance is not satisfactory, then surely this is the responsibility of the manager. There is no argument that the performance of a department or business should be the responsibility of the leader. However, the manager is usually not the root cause of the problem; the causes are usually deeper than that. As a former Toyota executive is reputed to have said, "We get brilliant results from average people operating and improving brilliant processes. Our competitors get mediocre results from brilliant people working around broken processes. Then, when they fail, they hire even more brilliant people [and still get worse results]."

Businesses should therefore strive continuously for process excellence. This includes processes for developing employees. The best source of leaders for your business should be from within your own company; existing employees will best understand your technology, your customers, their fellow employees, and your culture. Therefore, you must focus on developing existing staff by providing them with training, new projects, new challenges, and constant feedback (not just the annual performance review—one of Deming's seven diseases).

When Things Go Wrong: Managing Poor Performance

But what if things go wrong? There is no doubt that action must be taken when performance slips. However, that action should be asking why, not who. Managers need problem-solving techniques that address the root causes of problems, and treat them as an opportunity to improve processes and prevent problem recurrence. This is how superior performance is achieved and sustained.

There will be occasions when we do have the wrong person in a leadership role and need to make changes. These are the individuals who do not learn from experience, who do not develop their employees, and who consistently fail to apply rigor in finding and addressing the root causes of problems and substandard performance. We should help these individuals develop the skills of a problem solver, but, unfortunately, some individuals are unable or unwilling to learn. These individuals are not suitable for leadership roles. Even if their short-term business performance meets minimum acceptable levels, when managers do not want to learn or are incapable of improving job performance, accept the sad but true fact that they will be a threat to the future performance of your business.

Too often, with our focus on short-term results and business outcomes rather than process control, individuals are promoted for making decisions quickly or for responding to short-term issues by restructuring, reorganizing, outsourcing, divesting, and acquiring, hiring, and firing. This kind of action is mistakenly regarded as leadership and is viewed as more effective than the slow and painstaking tasks of solving problems using the scientific method and developing employees. The originators of Lean Thinking take a long-term view of developing people. "Some might debate whether people are born with talent, or whether talent is developed. Toyota's stance is clear—give us the seeds of talent and we will plant them, water and nurture the seedlings, and eventually harvest the fruits of our labor."[2]

Key Points in Chapter 6

- Very small manufacturers will tend to have only two layers of management, and managers generally work as front-line leaders or supervisors. Larger companies introduce middle management layers.
- The structure of middle management should, where possible, align with products or value streams rather than processes. This aligns the

motivation of managers with the need of the whole value stream, rather than just their respective departments.

■ Production teams should be kept to between seven and twelve employees to ensure that team members are properly supported.
■ Titles for team leaders are not important in the scheme of things. Use titles that work best for your business and beware of titles that are confusing or misleading.
■ Take care when recruiting new people. Be thorough, give consideration to internal candidates, always check references, and if you get it wrong and hire the wrong person—act quickly.
■ Avoid excessive hiring and firing, if you can. Constant turnover damages business performance.

References

1. Deming, W.E. 2000. *Out of the Crisis*. Boston, MA: MIT Press.
2. Liker, J.K. and Meier, D.P. 2007. *Toyota Talent: Developing Your People the Toyota Way*. New York: McGraw Hill.

Chapter 7

Measuring Success: Selecting the Right Metrics

What You Will Learn in This Chapter

- The importance of "keeping score in real time" of your business rather than relying only on monthly financial results that are weeks old
- Selecting the right metrics for your factory
- Choosing metrics that your team will understand, measure, and improve
- Selecting simple production metrics for processing manufacturing, where output is measured in a unit of measure such as meters, kilograms, or liters
- Metrics for non-manufacturing functions
- The importance of *delivery in full and on time (DIFOT)* and *overall equipment effectiveness (OEE)* as measures, and how to measure them correctly

Keeping Score in Real Time

Imagine a game of soccer without a score. The players compete for 90 minutes but nobody records the number of goals during the game, so at game's end nobody knows who won or lost. Imagine instead that game scores are tallied at the end of each month, and the cumulative scores are announced in the middle of the following month. I am sure you agree that this would be a fairly pointless exercise for the players and for the fans.

However, as you have already guessed, this is the way many businesses are run: business performance results are available 2 or 3 weeks after the end of the current month. The effect of this approach is similar to the soccer example above. By the time results are published, it is too late to correct the damage already done.

Now let's consider how scores in sporting contests are truly used. The score is recorded in real time, and teams and managers respond to every change in the course of the game. In addition to the score, however, a soccer team collects a huge range of statistics, such as percentage share of ball possession, share of territory, number of passes, fouls, and so on. These metrics are rightly seen as pointers to the team's overall performance and predictors of the likelihood of scoring goals and future success. A team that does not have possession of the ball and spends the game in its own half of the field is unlikely to score goals. Likewise in business, *if we can measure performance as closely as possible to real time, then we can respond quickly to poor performance, take effective corrective actions, and minimize losses.* By identifying and measuring the key drivers of business performance, we can ensure that we put our business in the best position to perform well.

What Are the Metrics in Your Business?

All businesses analyze some metrics, if only profit-and-loss and sales. However, many businesses publish a huge number of metrics. In one large company I once worked for, the finance manager set about collecting all the different metrics that were being used by managers within the business. In that one division alone, there were over 450 business metrics being collected. This is a recipe for confusion. The collection and reporting of so many measures represents a huge waste of time and effort (and cost).

So, the question becomes: What do you need to measure? Unfortunately, there is no universal solution. You need to answer that question for your own company. The starting point should be your business strategy. What are the high-level goals that your business needs to achieve? These are usually expressed in terms of financial measurements such as profit, return on assets, revenue, and working capital, as well as governance measures such as safety, employee turnover, and quality (both cost and performance data). You cannot win soccer games by just focusing on the score and not considering the underlying drivers of the score. Likewise in business, you need to

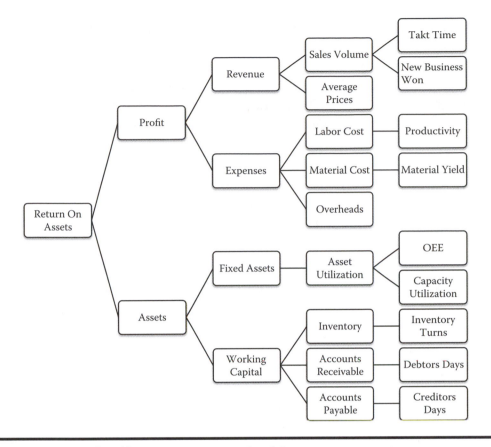

Figure 7.1 Example of how upstream metrics drive return on assets.

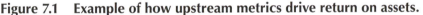

consider what the drivers are of your top-level metrics. Figure 7.1 shows how lower-level metrics can drive one top-level metric—return on assets.

As you can see in Figure 7.1, one can quickly build a big list of metrics. The challenge then is to select the right metrics to drive improvement without measuring too many things and creating confusion.

Select the Most Important Metrics to Focus On

There are always lots of things to do in business but it is important to choose the things that are most important to support the company's business strategy. We find that most managers can only effectively focus on improving a small number of metrics, perhaps no more than three or four. Therefore, how do you choose the right metrics?

Again, it pays to start with the company's strategic goal, and then drill down the strategic goal into concrete terms of how that goal applies to your individual particular team. For example, if the strategic goal is to grow revenue and you are a production manager, it is unlikely you will have much influence on pricing or on the amount of new business won. However, you could influence output. Therefore, in the production departments, your daily score might be output in units per hour or (as explained in Chapter 6), your ability to meet *takt* time. Next, you set output targets, ideally per hour, or perhaps every shift or every day if hourly measurement is too difficult. This becomes your goal. Team leaders record the scores. If production does not meet the target, the team leader is expected to analyze the cause, take action to prevent a repeat of the lost production, and also take steps, if possible, to catch up on the lost production.

The simple metric of how much is produced is a very good start. However, over time, the production manager might find that the same factors consistently lead to nonachievement of targets. For example, defective output or downtime leads to loss of production. This then might lead to measurement of the number of defects per hour or production downtime expressed in minutes. Analyzing further, the production manager might find that long setups are a key driver of downtime and therefore measure setup time in minutes. Perhaps we perform additional analysis and discover that the major cause of downtime is labor shortages. You might consider adding employee attendance as a further metric. Using this example, the production team would have five metrics:

1. Output in units, measured against an hourly target
2. Defects in units, measured for each hour
3. Downtime in minutes, measured for each hour or for the shift
4. Setup time in minutes, measured for each setup
5. Employee attendance, measured perhaps as the number of employees absent each day

You will notice that these are all very simple metrics. They can all be measured by either counting (output, defects, and attendance) or measuring time (downtime and setup time). *Many business metrics are expressed as ratios or percentages. In our experience, these are more difficult to understand and more difficult to collect, particularly by front-line employees.*

Typically, if a metric requires complex calculations, it should be collected using a computer, require centralized calculation, and therefore is likely available only as a historical measure, rather than measured in real-time or at short intervals (e.g., hourly). Simple counting or timing metrics, on the other hand, can be collected on the shop floor, recorded on the shop floor, and action taken quickly to solve problems when encountering substandard performance.

The role of the manager becomes similar to the role of a soccer coach: tracking the score, observing the play, and monitoring the statistics in real time as the game progresses, then afterward, coaching the team and solving problems to improve performance.

Develop a Simple Measure of Production Output

In many manufacturing companies, measuring output is not as easy as counting the number of filing cabinets (or the number of cars coming off an assembly line). In a paint or chemical factory, for example, measuring units of 1-liter cans means something completely different than measuring 10-liter cans. The output in units of the smaller product might be much greater but the larger can will represent more volume output and more value. Likewise in a machine shop, a unit might be a simple cylindrical bush, while the next unit might be a complex casting with multiple machining operations, followed by painting and assembly.

Sometimes a common unit of measure can be established. Many chemical processes, for example, apply a bulk measure such as liters or kilograms that can be used to measure the flow and control the rate of flow at each production point. In this case, *takt* time might convert to a rate expressed in liters or kilograms per hour, and you can level production using that measurement.

In jobbing or small batch production environments we often find that the number of batches or jobs is the key driver of activity. Each batch or job requires materials to be assembled, machinery changed over, and documentation prepared. Therefore, in those businesses we often find that the number of batches or jobs is the best measure of output. Naturally we always try to reduce batch size, but by focusing on managing the flow of jobs or batches, we are much better able to control the flow through the factory than to try to compare apples with oranges when managing unit output. We therefore calculate *takt* time based on the number of batches or jobs. In the example described above, if we were doing 10 jobs per day, our working time would be 420 minutes per day, and *takt* time would be 42 minutes per job.

Because all jobs are *not* the same, you cannot apply *takt* time as rigorously as you apply it when managing discrete units. Perhaps the most relevant figure is the daily target of 10 jobs. Setting a target of 10 batches or jobs a day can be immensely valuable in balancing your workload throughout your factory. The aim is to ensure that each process step completed its 10 jobs every day. Balancing the way you release work to the factory can reduce imbalances in the type of work. For example, not releasing all the time-consuming jobs at once or not releasing all the easy jobs at once, but mixing them to balance the workload.

Metrics for Other Functions

Thus far I have discussed front-line production metrics, but what about other parts of the business? The approach taken is the same: Understand the strategic goals and determine and install localized metrics that will drive the achievement of those goals. Using the same example shown above, if the company were aiming to increase revenue, the key warehouse metric would be how much product the warehouse can ship. Another metric might be the number of orders processed per day. Why not hourly? Because it may not be possible to level warehouse output at short intervals due to cycles of product dispatch and delivery, so daily metrics are probably more feasible than hourly.

Driving the number of orders processed might be the availability of store employees as well as the number of picking errors encountered and corrected. Loading and unloading of trucks might be a key constraint (or cost), and therefore average truck loading or unloading times, or truck waiting times, might be important. For this type of metric, it may be impractical to measure the time on site for every single truck. Therefore, a standard might be to set that "all trucks should depart loaded within 1 hour of arrival." The number of vehicles falling outside that standard could then be measured. Again we focus on metrics that can be counted or timed, thereby eliminating the complexity of more advanced metrics and applying metrics that shop employees can readily understand.

For the supply chain team, its job is to ensure that the finished goods are available to sell and raw materials are available to make scheduled production. A favorite finished goods metric of mine is the number of stocked items showing no stock on hand. This is usually very easy to measure with a system-generated report, can be reported at any time, and is a good predictor of delivery failure.

Likewise, the number of production interruptions due to material shortages can provide a good indicator of raw material availability. Of course, the supply chain is usually constrained by the amount of inventory it can hold, and in this case, inventory turns (a more complex metric representing the number of times inventory turns over annually) is an important metric. Measuring just inventory value is simpler but can be deceiving because if sales are increasing, then unless supply chain parameters change, inventory will increase proportionally.

Up to this point, I have emphasized the need for simple metrics that do not involve ratios. However, for almost every manufacturing business, there are two ratio metrics that are important: (1) delivery in full and on time (DIFOT) and (2) overall equipment effectiveness (OEE).

Delivery in Full and on Time (DIFOT): The Most Abused Metric in Manufacturing

The business of manufacturing is fulfilling customers' needs by providing them with the high-quality products they want, when they want them, and in quantities they want. It is therefore surprising how many small and medium-sized enterprises (SMEs) do not measure their performance in achieving this basic business metric. It is, however, somewhat less surprising that those that do measure it often delude themselves with doctored or inaccurate data. On the surface, it seems simple to calculate. Take the number of orders that have been delivered on the customer's required due date and divide it by the number of orders dispatched in total (including those that were dispatched incomplete or late). The result is a percentage. For example if we shipped 100 orders and 90 were delivered on the customer's required date and in full, then our DIFOT would be 90%. Simple, isn't it?

Unfortunately, the devil with this metric is in the detail. What if the customer's required date is unreasonable? For example, the standard lead-time is 1 week but the customer asks for delivery of a rush order the next day. What if your process does not produce the exact customer quantity? For example, many batch processes such as plastics extrusion or printing normally have small losses so the quantity produced may vary slightly from the quantity ordered. Often, contracts allow for these slight overruns or underruns. What if your customer requests an early due date but willingly agrees to a later delivery date when you ask them for more time? There is another practical problem: It is often difficult to measure and control the actual time of delivery to the customer's warehouse. Most companies will measure whether the goods are shipped on time and assume that the goods will then be delivered on time, which has the potential of causing dissatisfied customers.

Resolving this problem has a purist approach and a practical approach. The purist approach is to say that on-time delivery means supplying the customer exactly the quantity it orders on the day it orders it. This is measured by the ratio of orders delivered (not shipped) on time and in full compared to the total number of orders shipped.

The more practical approach is what I recommend most companies use (or at least start with). First, it is important to understand the service-level agreement (SLA) with the customer. This should state the agreed order lead-time and whether the customer will accept a quantity that exceeds the order (as in the example of batch process manufacturing). On-time delivery is then measured against the delivery date agreed upon with the customer at the time the order is placed. If the delivery date is subsequently pushed back further, then this should be considered a late delivery, *regardless of whether or not the customer agreed to the change.* If you want to be a bit tougher, you can restrict the negotiation of dates to apply only within the agreed-upon lead-time. Therefore, if you have an agreed-upon 4-week lead-time and the customer wants a 2-week lead-time instead, but you subsequently agree to a 3-week lead-time, this can be accommodated, but you would not be permitted to negotiate a lead-time longer than 4 weeks. If you did, it would constitute a late delivery, whether or not the customer agreed to the delay. *In the realm of quantity for batch production, provided the delivery is within the tolerance agreed upon with the customer (say, ±5%), this should be considered delivery in full.*

Overriding these considerations is the perspective of the customer. Many large customers measure the DIFOT of their suppliers. When this occurs, it is vital that you understand how you are being measured and what your performance is. Ideally, you should align your own measurement of DIFOT with your customer's measurement. I have seen several companies proudly boast a DIFOT of 98%+, while their customers rate their performance much lower. These companies are deluding themselves.

It is highly risky for your business to allow gaps—between how your customer measures you and how you measure yourself—go unresolved and unexplained.

Eventually, you may be surprised when the customer you thought you had a great delivery record with tells you that he is looking for another supplier.

In terms of what is acceptable for DIFOT, I like to invert the measure and think about the frequency of delivery failures. Therefore at 80% DIFOT, one delivery in five will be late or incomplete. In my experience, this is unacceptable to most businesses. Usually, a minimum of one delivery miss in twenty (or potentially one miss per month) is the least customers will expect. This corresponds to 95% DIFOT, and in my experience is usually the ***minimum*** that you should aim for.

Overall Equipment Effectiveness (OEE)

Overall equipment effectiveness (OEE) is a measure of the performance of the machines within a business. It is the foundation metric of total productive maintenance (TPM), the Lean approach to maintaining optimum machine performance. Good machine performance measured by OEE is important both for increasing productivity and for providing a stable process, where machines always run when they need to run, and downtime is minimized. OEE is another metric that gets abused a lot. Companies often delude themselves about their performance. OEE is measured as a percentage ratio of time and is usually calculated by multiplying three other ratios together:

$$OEE = (Equipment\ Availability\%) \times (Performance\ Efficiency\%)$$
$$\times (Quality\ Rate\%)$$

These three ratios in turn are measured as follows:

■ Equipment Availability is the proportion of time when a machine is planned to run and is actually running as opposed to stopped. This ratio is calculated as

Equipment availability =

$$\frac{(Net\ available\ time) - (Unplanned\ downtime + Setup\ time)}{(Net\ available\ time)} \times 100\%$$

Net available time = (Total time) − (Planned downtime)*

---

* I have heard differing views whether setup times constitute "planned" downtime. In my opinion you are better to limit "planned downtime" to time when the plant is not operating at all or the machine is not crewed to run (e.g., if the factory runs three shifts, but the machine is only crewed to run two, then I would call the third shift planned downtime). If you define setups as "planned downtime" then you remove the incentive to reduce setup times.

■ Performance Efficiency measures the output of the machine when it is actually running. Is it running at its standard rate, or is it running slower or having a lot of short stoppages?

$$\text{Performance efficiency} = \frac{(\text{Standard cycle time}) \times (\text{Total \# parts produced})}{(\text{Net available time}) \times 100\%}$$

■ Quality Rate measures the machine output losses due to producing defects and is calculated as

$$\text{Quality rate} = \frac{(\text{Total \# parts produced}) - (\text{Total \# of defects produced})}{(\text{Total \# of parts produced}) \times 100\%}$$

Note that in calculating the Quality Rate and Performance Efficiency, the total parts produced is the total output, including both good and defective parts.

The OEE measured this way is a very powerful measure. Care must be exercised when defining terms to avoid problems similar to those encountered with DIFOT. The two dangerous areas are defining the standard cycle time and unplanned downtime. The standard cycle time should be the "nameplate" cycle time of the machine (or the tool in the case of injection molding). It is defined as the best possible cycle time expected when the machine or product was first installed.

Often, companies choose soft standards, which might represent an average or typical cycle time. Some companies have a misguided view that running machines at full speed wears them out—they were designed to run fast!

It is possible to fudge unplanned downtime or setup time by not including machine downtime when those machines are down for repairs. Accepting soft standards like that means that you are accepting waste in your process, and you may never find the opportunity to improve machine uptime. In our experience, most companies will find that their OEE, when they first measure it, is less than 50%. Treat this as great news because it means you have lots of opportunity for improvement. On the other hand, the companies we see that claim an OEE greater than 95% are almost certainly deluding themselves and covering up significant improvement potential.

Key Points in Chapter 7

■ Timely and relevant metrics are as important for a manufacturing business as the scores and game statistics are for a soccer match. Without them, you cannot improve and the game becomes pretty meaningless.

■ Select metrics that align with your company's strategic goals. It makes sense to start with the top-level goals and then identify drivers at each level of the organization that impact the achievement of those top-level goals.

■ Choose a maximum of three or four simple metrics for each function or department.

■ Measure as frequently as possible—hopefully every hour for output against target.

■ Where possible, select metrics that can be collected by counting or by measuring time. The point is to avoid complex ratios wherever possible. The more complex, the harder it is for front-line employees to record, use, and understand the data.

■ For custom and process manufacturing, measuring output can be more complex than just counting the number of units completed. In these cases, simple alternative units of measure should be developed. For many custom manufacturers, batch processes, and jobbing shops, tracking the number of jobs is a simple and effective measure of output and activity.

■ Two basic ratios that most manufacturing businesses need to measure are delivery on time and in full (DIFOT) and overall equipment effectiveness (OEE). If you are not already measuring these, you should consider starting to do so.

■ Both DIFOT and OEE are frequently subject to manipulation. Manipulating metrics to improve the results may make you feel good, but will limit improvement opportunities and hide problems.

Chapter 8

What Do I Make Next? The Keys to Production Planning

What You Will Learn in This Chapter

- How to control the flow of work in your factory to avoid big backlogs and bottlenecks
- How to achieve and maintain balance between the various production processes in your factory
- How to plan and manage your capacity
- The problems of using an ERP (enterprise requirements planning) system for planning, and why ERPs are not the answer for most SME (small and medium-sized enterprise) manufacturers

Controlling the Release of Work to the Factory: What Goes In Must Come Out

Planning and scheduling production is an area in which most manufacturers (usually aided and abetted by eager software vendors) greatly overcomplicate things. Once you have defined your single pacemaker process (see Chapter 4), planning production should be particularly simple.

We know that customer demand is equal to *takt* time. Therefore, we need to release orders to production at a rate that enables us to keep up with, but not exceed, the *takt* time. For example, if the *takt* time is 1 hour, we need to release one product or job to the pacemaker process every hour. Typically,

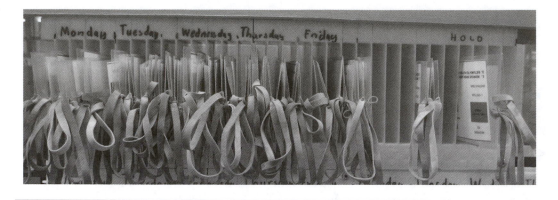

Figure 8.1 Example of a load-leveling box in Branach Manufacturing. Each card represents the requirement to manufacture a ladder.

we will spread the jobs throughout the day, releasing planned increments. The method we often use to do this is a load-leveling box or, as it is often called, a *Heijunka* box (Figure 8.1).

The load-leveling box at Branach Manufacturing shown in Figure 8.1 controls the rate of kitting. Kitting of custom parts (assembling kits of parts for specific orders) is the pacemaker process. Kits are supplied in FIFO (first-in-first-out) order to assembly. As you can see, there are four slots for each day, and each slot holds a batch of four products. The worker takes each batch and picks the kit of parts for that batch. Progress through the week and the level of backlog were clearly visible through the number of jobs in the slots.

As explained previously, in many jobbing shops, the best measurement needed to control production is the number of jobs. So if the average output is 10 jobs per day, then we should set up a load-leveling box with 10 slots for each day. This is a really powerful concept. Often we find that companies put no thought into how they release their work onto the shop floor. If they become busy, they tend to release all their outstanding jobs to the shop floor in the mistaken belief that the more orders they release to the production system, the more orders they will pump out efficiently. But in many manufacturing businesses, the upstream process is highly automated and has an output that can easily exceed the required production rate—for example, the corrugator or printer in box manufacturing, the CNC lathe in gear manufacturing, or the filling machine in food or pharmaceutical plants. Downstream processes are often slower and less automated (such as packing, gluing, welding, and assembly). Companies often focus on keeping the big, expensive automated machines upstream busy, and forget the consequences of poor workflow. Even when the customer only needs 10 jobs and the downstream processes can only handle 10 jobs, work will continue to be released to the first process to keep it busy. As you can well imagine, this approach creates a buildup of work-in-progress (WIP). *In manufacturing, we get paid for the jobs we finish, not the jobs we start.*

As you increase your backlog of WIP by starting more and more jobs, the lead-time increases. Let's say that you get busy and you release 20 jobs per day for a week. You only finish 10 jobs per day and so after just 1 week, you have increased WIP by 50 jobs or 5 days. The so-called efficiency of your first process might look great, but a new customer coming along with a new order will now have to wait an extra 5 days for delivery.

Eventually you will need to slow your releases of work and reduce the backlog, thus requiring the plant to increase the rate of your *slowest* process. These are usually labor-intensive and/or space-intensive processes, and increasing the output usually involves overtime. If you decide to run every Saturday to catch up, you will finish an extra 10 jobs per week but it will still take 5 weeks for you to reduce your backlog down to the level it was when you increased the number of start orders. *Most importantly, you are still only selling 10 units per day, so the overtime you need to deliver customer orders will not deliver increased sales. It will, instead, drive excess costs straight to your bottom line.*

Getting Processes Back in Balance and Keeping Them That Way

Unbalanced processes and poor production planning cause this problem and, as consultants, we see it every day. Fortunately, it is easy to fix. There are a few basic rules to follow:

- Release work to production at *takt* time or your target rate of jobs per day—never more, never less. Use a load-leveling box to release the work at an even rate.
- Remember that your process lead time (the time it takes you to make the product from start to finish) needs to be significantly less than the customer lead time (the time you promise your customer). This will give you a buffer to allow for variations in demand.
- Try and balance the release of work so that you don't release all the "easy" jobs or all the "hard" jobs at once. Mixing them up will level the workload in your factory.

■ Measure the output of every process against the *takt* time or target rate. If the process falls behind the target rate, take action such as overtime or applying additional resources to catch up. If it gets ahead, stop and do not produce anymore. (Yes, even if it is the biggest and most expensive machine in the factory, stop and switch off the big machine when it has made enough to meet target rates.)

■ Use FIFO to minimize the buildup of inventory between each process, and enforce the FIFO rules (see Chapter 4 for an explanation of FIFO).

Don't Start What You Can't Finish

Another problem companies have when they get busy is pushing incomplete orders into the production queue even before raw materials are delivered or before design is fully specified. Inevitably what happens is that the job reaches a point in the process and cannot continue until the material, customer specifications, or design drawings are completed. Making products that cannot be completed or sold is a waste of scarce production capacity. The inevitable result is an unnecessary buildup of WIP inventory. A lot of management time will be wasted expediting what is missing.

The Toyota Production System stipulates that we should have direct customer–supplier connections with simple, unambiguous ways to send requests and receive responses. Before we pump orders into the production system, we need to know what we are making (finished and complete designs and specifications), and have the tools and materials to produce it. Remember that production is the customer of engineering, purchasing, and sales, and it is the job of those functions to provide accurate and complete information and materials to production to enable timely processing of customer orders. If they do not provide the information, then the customer (production) is entitled to say, "No, I cannot make that until you provide me what I need." This approach sounds harsh but it works. It is entirely reasonable to ask customers to tell you exactly what they want before you start to make it. If they don't, both you (as the manufacturer) and your customers suffer.

Likewise, by demanding service from their internal suppliers, and not accepting incomplete information and materials, production quickly educates sales, engineering, and purchasing of the necessity to supply complete information if they want customer orders completed correctly and on time. In return, when the customer–supplier relationship is reversed, sales can expect the customer to get the right product at the right time in the right quantity from production.

Planning Capacity

Capacity planning is another subject that companies tend to make massively complicated. Many try to balance the capacity of every production process. If you have struggled to make this work, I suggest you pick up a copy of *The Goal,*[1] which explains in a very entertaining way why you should only plan your bottleneck processes—or pacemaker processes, as I call it.

If you have a single pacemaker process and have a set daily rate of output, then capacity planning becomes very easy. It is simply a matter of filling the available production slots. If in our running example, your production rate is 10 jobs per day, it becomes a matter of deciding which 10 jobs to start. This can be done very easily on a spreadsheet.

Of course, it is likely that 10 jobs per day may not always be your demand quantity. A rolling 12-month forecast helps us see the trends in our data, both growth and decline over time, as well as seasonal trends and plans for them. You can calculate the monthly rate that you need to meet your forecast demand. This 12-month forecast is different from the type of forecast I discuss below. For capacity planning, you only need to forecast at the monthly level. Also it is usually enough to just forecast at the value stream level and it is not necessary to forecast every single product variant. You just need to know how many units or jobs the line will need to run, you can assume an "average" product mix to keep things simple.

For example, let's say your forecast shows sales increasing by 20% over the summer months. To meet the new set of requirements, you need to increase output from 10 to 12 jobs per day. To fulfill the expanded forecast, you must determine what, if any, additional machines, shifts, or employees are needed to meet this additional demand. Perhaps it might be possible to level that demand and start building inventory in the spring, thus enabling the plant to run for 6 months at 11 jobs per day and reduce the impact on capacity. In either case, it is a straightforward calculation and one that can be done without the use of complex planning tools. The case study described on the following pages illustrates how a customer was able to more effectively manage his capacity and demand this way rather than with the more burdensome and complex materials requirements planning (MRP) software.

Will a Software System Improve Your Production Planning and On-Time Delivery?

Most SMEs will reach a point where planning production and keeping track of what is in production becomes a challenge. Sadly, the first temptation of many manufacturers when that situation arises is to look for a software solution. I think the logic is that "If I can automate my production processes, then I can also automate my business processes." Unfortunately, things are not that simple. Software will not improve how well your factory meets its customers' needs. People improve customer delivery performance, not computers. If you have problems with planning and on-time delivery, adding software will probably make it worse by automating the chaos! We recommend that the first step for companies is to value stream map their production and supply chain processes (see Chapter 4). Next, find the root causes of their delivery problems and then implement a future state map to fix those problems. The simple Lean visual techniques such as scheduling at one point and load-leveling boxes are usually more effective and responsive than complex computer-based scheduling systems.

What's Wrong with Using an ERP System to Plan Production?

Most business software systems these days are described (rightly or wrongly) as ERP (enterprise requirements planning) systems. That means they have the capability to plan the resource needs of the enterprise: labor, materials, and machines. However, this approach has one fatal flaw: it relies on the forecast, and forecasts are seldom accurate. This, not surprisingly, is because people are not very good at predicting the future.

I like to make an analogy using the science of weather forecasting. Let's say it is October and we are trying to forecast the weather in January. There is some information readily available. We know, for example, that January weather in Australia is likely to be hotter and dryer than in October (the opposite is true in the Northern Hemisphere).

This is useful information to know as it might affect some long-range decisions such as what clothes you buy and when you plan to take your holidays. But what about the weather in Melbourne, Australia, on January 26? Even the bravest forecaster would hesitate to give anything more than a broad range of outcomes for the weather on a specific day that far in advance. Even if we narrowed the time horizon to a fortnight, providing an accurate forecast down to the day is an exercise in futility. *The point here is that the value of forecasts depends on the time horizon and the level of detail that you attempt to forecast.*

Using a forecast of limited accuracy to decide via an ERP system what products to make on a given week, or worse, a given day, and to make that forecast weeks or months in advance, is likely to mean you will be making the wrong product in the wrong quantities at the wrong time to meet your customers' needs.

The ERP experts would then argue that to overcome this, you need fixed and firm planning horizons and you need to educate your customers in the need to forecast and then stick to their forecast. But what if your customers are not prepared to provide you with this information? Or what if your competitors do not require it? You may find yourself at a competitive disadvantage.

You may well need business software; just don't be tempted by the mirage that you can use it to plan your factory's production schedule and the materials that schedule requires based on a forecast. In my experience, the forecast-to-replenish model simply does not work effectively in most manufacturing businesses. It typically leads to higher inventory, longer lead-times, poorer DIFOT, as well as a huge amount of work trying to feed the system with accurate data, and a lot of excess time wasted expediting orders. It is far more effective to go with the simple Lean approaches to planning as described in this chapter. The following case study provides an excellent example of a customer that was heavily committed to the ERP approach and, with TXM's support, switched to a Lean pull system for planning. That customer achieved dramatic improvements in lead-time and inventory reduction, and substantial improvements in the DIFOT metric.

Case Study: Planning a Seasonal Operation: From ERP to Pull

Our customer was a medium-sized paint manufacturer. They had invested heavily in an ERP system and used the MRP functionality in this system to plan production. Using MRP first involves establishing a set of master data in your system for every customer, product, part, and material used, and asset employed. That includes maintaining accurate bills of materials and routings for every job. In addition, a set of master production schedule (MPS) settings are established, which includes data about optimum batch sizes, lead-times, and safety stock requirements.

The paint company used this information to develop a weekly forecast and loaded the information into the ERP system. The MRP function ran overnight and scheduled the required production time, materials, and inventory to meet the forecast requirements. In Lean manufacturing terms, we call this *push scheduling*, where the supply of raw materials and WIP are pushed to the next production step in anticipation of future demand.

The problem, of course, becomes forecasting demand for every product (SKU) every week. Despite a lot of effort, high inventory, and relatively good forecast accuracy, the customer still had constant problems with shortages and rush orders in production.

Working with TXM, the customer mapped its supply chain using a value stream map (see Chapter 4). The value stream map focused on reducing the lead-time from when the need for a production batch is triggered to when the finished batch is put back into stock. The lead-time was reduced from around 3 weeks to approximately 5 days. Batch sizes were also reduced to enable the business to cycle through products more quickly. Where necessary, they focused on reducing setup times so that the smaller batches could be made without impacting efficiency (Figure 8.2).

Figure 8.2 Paint factory production manager (left) leading a setup time reduction exercise for a paint can labeling machine. Reducing setup times was a key enabler for reducing batch sizes.

The trigger for the inventory was changed from forecast to usage by establishing a *Kanban* system. The daily sales of products became the trigger to replace stock. A report was sent from the distribution center to the factory each day. This report told the production planner which products she needed to manufacture next. The level of finished goods stock was determined from the lead-time needed to replenish the batch and the batch size. *As a result, finished inventory was reduced by 30%, and shortages were reduced to almost zero.*

The challenge for a paint factory forecast is that people do not paint their houses in winter. Demand is highly seasonal as shown in Figure 8.3. Notice that sales in the peak month of March are about 50% higher than sales in August. If the business ran purely on a *Kanban* system, stock levels would likely be too low to cover peak demand and too high in the quiet months. Also, the demand on production in the peak months would be much higher, meaning the factory would need to have a higher output of batches in those months compared to the quiet months and would need to plan to adjust labor accordingly.

Fortunately, the business already had a sales and operations planning process. Consequently, although MRP and the weekly forecast were abandoned, the monthly forecast and sales and operations planning process were retained. This enabled production to plan labor requirements for both the peak months

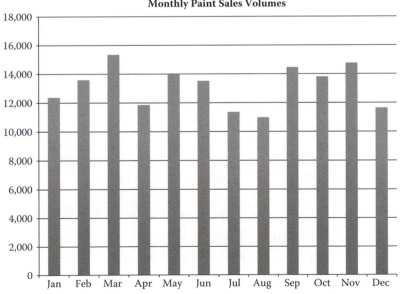

Figure 8.3   Graph depicting the seasonality of paint sales throughout the year.

and the slow months, while maintaining both lead-times and efficiency. For planning purposes, the factory adjusted inventory by releasing more *Kanban* batches to production before the peak months and removing *Kanbans* (by not replacing them when they were triggered) in the quiet months. This ensured not only available inventory to meet peak demand, but also a corresponding drop in production when demand fell after the painting season.

The sales and operations planning system also proved invaluable the year after our project, when the company won a large one-off supply contract. They were able to factor the one-off in their monthly sales and operations planning process, thereby ensuring that production could ramp up to meet the one-off demand while maintaining high levels of service to regular customers.

Key Points in Chapter 8

■ Plan production at one crucial point in the production process. This is called the *pacemaker* and can be found by working backward, checking production flow starting in shipping and working backward until you reach the point where orders no longer flow downstream, and are instead composed of materials pulled from upstream processes.

■ A load-leveling box, or *Heijunka* box, is a very effective tool to control the regular release of work to the production line at regular intervals.

■ If you believe that you cannot implement a load-leveling box, you should at least limit the release of work at a constant daily rate.

■ Calculate the daily rate or *takt* time, and make sure you review and, if necessary, adjust the rate up or down each month based on expected changes in overall forecast demand.

■ Ensure that all processes have the capability to meet *takt* time, and only release work at *takt* time, *even if the pacemaker process is capable of completing more than that rate*. If a bottleneck process cannot meet *takt* time, you will not be able to meet your customer demand and therefore you must somehow increase the output of that bottleneck process by improving the performance of that machine, working the machine overtime, assigning other machinery capable of processing the same parts, or some other mechanism to relieve the bottleneck.

■ Remember that what matters is the amount of production or the number of jobs your factory finishes, *not* the number it starts. Avoid building up big backlogs of WIP by balancing throughput at each process to meet the daily rate.

■ Avoid starting work you cannot finish by making sure that you have complete specification details, and all materials are on site before you release the job to production.

■ Develop a simple capacity plan that translates the forecast into forward requirements, and schedules the release of work at the pacemaker. This can further highlight whether or not you will meet production due dates and ensure that you adjust production rates and inventory levels up or down as demand changes.

■ Computerized planning systems (ERPs) sound exciting but are generally not effective in SME manufacturers. This is because they rely on a level of forecast detail and accuracy that is impossible to achieve. Simple Lean planning systems provide lower inventory and better on-time delivery.

Reference

1. Goldratt, E.M. and Cox, J. 1992. *The Goal: A Process of Ongoing Improvement.* Great Barrington, MA: North River Press.

Chapter 9

What I Need When I Need It: Managing Materials

What You Will Learn in This Chapter

- The likely reasons your business keeps running out of materials
- Why your suppliers are probably not the major causes of your shortages
- How to develop a service-level agreement (SLA) with suppliers
- How to develop a simple system for material supply that will reduce your inventory *and* reduce your shortages
- What a *Kanban* system is, the different types of *Kanban* or pull systems, and how you can apply them in your business

A Typical Material Supply Problem: How It Happens

Picture the following scenario: You now have everything in place for your Lean manufacturing operation. You have a great production flow that has been translated into a highly efficient factory layout. You have hired a great team, and you have a simple but effective system for planning your production. Your first products are almost ready to roll off your Lean production cell...and there is a holdup. A critical component that you need to complete the product has not arrived in time. Everything stops. The workforce stops working, and team leaders run around trying to find something for the workers to do. Eventually, after several phone calls and much hand-wringing, the missing parts arrive, production starts up again, the product is completed and delivered, and you heave a sigh of relief.

Later that day, you walk through your fully stocked warehouse thinking about how, with an average of 3 months' worth of raw material inventory on hand, could you have run out of that part? You silently curse your supplier and think about firing your purchasing manager. Instead, you decide to increase the safety stock on that part just in case.

Unfortunately, the scenario described above is all too common. One major customer of ours measured its shortages and found that it had over 100 part shortages per day, which meant that *every product it made was likely to be delayed by at least one shortage. In most cases, excessive inventory and constant shortages go hand in hand.*

Another company we were engaged to help had 140 days of raw material inventory. In fact, they had so much inventory that they were paying a six-figure annual amount in container demurrage, as they did not have enough space to unpack all the containers of imported inventory it had ordered. *Despite this, the number one cause of downtime and missed deliveries was material shortages, and they also had an annual six-figure bill for airfreight to expedite delivery of parts.* How could this unlikely combination of problems possibly happen?

Not every company gets in as much trouble as the two companies described above, but it is not uncommon for excess inventory to correlate with part shortages. *Problems with having the right part in the right place at the right time are almost universal among manufacturers.* "But, hang on a minute," I hear you say. "Isn't there software out there that can fix this problem?" In almost every case where I have seen supply problems, the customer has *already* invested hundreds of thousands or even millions of dollars in an enterprise requirements planning (ERP) system.

The Old Forecast Problem

As explained in Chapter 8, the limitation with ERP systems is the accuracy of the forecast; and while forecasts may be accurate enough to plan overall capacity on a monthly level, they will usually not be accurate enough to determine when materials must be delivered. Therefore, if you rely on forecast-driven ordering of parts, you are likely to end up with the wrong parts at the wrong time in the wrong quantities. This means you cannot produce what you planned. Therefore, you produce another product

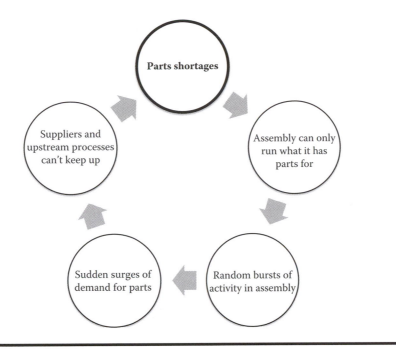

Figure 9.1 The vicious cycle driving "roadrunner" production.

in its place, assuming you have an adequate supply of materials available. Unfortunately, this solution is inadequate; by making the products out of sequence, you bring forward requirements for parts used in the second product, and you soon run out of them too. Your labor is then moved to other operations where materials are available. We call this "roadrunner" production because the plant will have random bursts of activity when material becomes available, and stops when parts run out. This cycle reminds me of the way the cartoon character, The Roadrunner, used to race off at high speed and then stop, only to go again. This leads to highly variable demand on upstream processes and suppliers who will struggle to cope. As a result, the problem of shortages just gets worse and worse, even when you are increasing safety stocks and ordering larger quantities. This becomes a "vicious" cycle as shown in Figure 9.1.

Unreliable Suppliers

Often upon meeting companies with major material shortage and excess inventory problems, they tell us how unreliable their suppliers are. "If only the suppliers would deliver on time, we would not have any shortages," they say.

I have analyzed this problem on many occasions for many different companies. What I normally find (about 80% of the time) is that the root causes of so-called supplier unreliability have nothing to do with the supplier and everything to do with how the buyer manages the suppliers. The thing to remember about suppliers is that they are independent businesses with a need to run their own operations and deliver the best possible service to *all* their customers (not just yours), and deliver an adequate return to their shareholders. Even—or perhaps especially—if your supplier is another division of your own company, it will have its own business goals independent of yours, and it is likely that you will not be its only customer. It is not in your supplier's interest to cause you problems; like any other business, the supplier's aim is to keep its customers happy, so the company is motivated to do its best to meet your needs. Given all this, what is going wrong?

Suppliers have their own processes and their own value stream that is independent of yours (unless you have included them in an extended value stream mapping process). This means they have lead-times they can reliably meet, minimum batch sizes that make sense for them, and a delivery schedule and process that fit their operational requirements. They also have suppliers of their own that have independent lead-times and requirements. If you are a giant company such as GM, Ford, or Chrysler, for example, you can dictate to your suppliers how you want them to run their businesses because chances are that those suppliers would go out of business without orders from the "Big Three." But this is a book about SME manufacturing, and it is unlikely your suppliers will be willing to completely redesign their businesses to fit your company's requirements. Under those circumstances, you need to persuade your suppliers that it is in their best interest to help you. I am surprised how many companies simply do not take this first step of asking their suppliers to help them resolve parts planning problems. There is nothing wrong with seeking expertise from all quarters. Some of the questions you might ask include

- What is their order lead-time? Back this up by reviewing their actual performance. Suppliers may either overpromise to win a sale or underpromise to give themselves an excessive time buffer. Try to get them to agree to something that is realistic, and then measure their performance in achieving it. Make sure your ordering process allows for this lead-time.
- What is their minimum order quantity? What are the consequences if you order smaller batch sizes? It will reduce your raw material and parts inventory, and the cost of ordering less may be minimal.

- Will your supplier hold an inventory of your parts for you to call for at short notice? This can really slash the level of inventory in your factory and greatly reduce the risk of shortages. I am sometimes criticized because that is not a Lean solution, as it simply moves inventory from your store to your suppliers. But in many cases it will suit suppliers to operate this way. For example, packaging suppliers can group print runs together and gain efficiencies on their machines rather than running each print variant individually to order.
- What delivery options do they offer? How often can they deliver to your site, and can they deliver at set times to level the activity in your receiving area? Can you arrange for goods to be picked up at the supplier's plant or warehouse by your freight provider?
- Would your monthly forecast help them plan capacity to meet your demand? In this case, you can share that information with them. *But make clear they are not to manufacture goods according to your forecast, or some suppliers may be tempted to rush off and manufacture a whole year's worth of your products.*

Once you have agreement about these rules of engagement with your supplier, you should document them in a service-level agreement (SLA). This is a written procedure, usually signed by both parties, that outlines how you are going to do business together. The SLA provides a valuable reference point and can greatly reduce difficulties in your relationship should questions arise. It is also a good idea to include some performance metrics in the document such as on-time delivery and quality metrics. *One caution: Make sure you and the supplier agree on how the metrics are measured.*

After completing the SLA, it is also a good idea to sign ongoing supply agreements with your key suppliers. In many cases, I find that companies have no formal relationship with their suppliers beyond a purchase order. Under those circumstances, it is impossible for suppliers to plan for your needs if they have no indication that the orders currently fulfilled are not your final ones. You do not need to commit to buy particular volumes, and you do not even need to commit to use the supplier exclusively, but a supply agreement will provide your suppliers with some confidence that your relationship will be an ongoing one. It is also likely that you can negotiate much better pricing and a better SLA if it comes with a commitment to ongoing business.

Developing a Plan for Every Part

You now know what you need to produce and when to produce it, and you know what your supplier can deliver, how frequently, and in what quantities. Next, you need a system to make sure that you order the right quantity of every material at the right time and hold the correct amount of inventory, avoid shortages, and minimize working capital. The starting point here is to develop a "Plan for Every Part" (PFEP). A PFEP is usually a spreadsheet that lists all your materials. It describes their key characteristics, inventory levels, how they will be stored, and how they will be replenished. For a detailed description of developing a PFEP (and managing materials generally), read a copy of *Making Materials Flow* by Harris, Harris, and Wilson.[1] Much of what I have to say is drawn from that excellent book.

To build your PFEP, start with a table in Excel® with all your material part codes and descriptions in the left-hand columns. Then progressively add columns to populate the data you need to control your materials. Typically, the type of data you need includes

- Supplier name (or supplier code in your business system)
- Minimum order quantity
- Supplier lead-time
- Ordering frequency (if this is fixed)
- Average usage (daily, weekly, or monthly usage); whatever the case, it needs to align with your ordering frequency
- Packaging type(s)
- Quantity per pack
- Packaging size (if relevant)
- Pack weight (if relevant)
- Type of storage (e.g., rack, shelving, or floor storage)
- Storage location
- Shelf life (if relevant)

From this data and supporting information, you calculate the inventory required and the frequency and quantity of orders and build a table similar to the one in Table 9.1.

You start with an assumption: that your method of replenishment will use a pull rather than push process. A pull system means ordering parts and materials to replenish the parts and materials already used. A push system, on the other hand, uses a forecast to calculate the quantities of materials you

Table 9.1   Example Input Data for a PFEP

		Plan for Every Part Example				
Stockcode	Description	Stockgroup 1	Supplier Name	Min	Max	Last Yr July 11 to Jun 12
DX4816	Cross Join 24 × 33 mm–1,200 mm	02. EXPOSED CEILING SYSTEMS	RSC–Ceilector	15,000	60,000	88,793
4246-60	Furring Duct 28 × 37 mm–6,000 mm	01. CONCE CEILING SYSTEMS	Walco Australia Pty Ltd	5,760	15,360	20,670
1655	Galv. Rod 5 mm–4,000 mm	03. CEILING SYSTEM ACCESSORIES	Steelex	800	6,400	22,781
9639-30	92 mm Truss 0.55–3,000 mm	06. STUD AND TRACK	Walco Australia Pty Ltd	200	600	10,704
8242	4,246 Perimeter Duct 28 mm–3,000 mm	01. CONCE CEILING SYSTEMS	Naxis	600	1,200	18,596
VT4819	Ventatec Cross Join 24 × 38 mm–1,200 mm	02. EXPOSED CEILING SYSTEMS	AMF Deckensysteme	1	10,000	15,821
DX3813	Main Join 24 × 38 mm–3,600 mm	02. EXPOSED CEILING SYSTEMS	RSC–Ceilector	3,000	12,000	13,998
3248-48	Primary Duct 25 mm–0.75–4,800 mm	01. CONCE CEILING SYSTEMS	Walco Australia Pty Ltd	200	600	9,399

continued

Table 9.1 (continued)   Example Input Data for a PFEP

Stockcode	Type	Buy Qty	Qty per Pallet	Height	Pallet Stack Height	Length	Weight (ea)	Pallet Weight kg	Lead-Time to Resupply (days)	Usage (12 months)	Daily Usage (220 days per yr)
			Pallet data							Consumption	
DX4816	Pallet	15,000	3,600	24	86,500	1,200	0.37	1,332	5	88,793	403.60
4,246-60	Pallet	240	240			6,000	3.01	722.4	3	26,640	121.09
1,655	Pallet	6,400	6,400			4,000	0.6	3,840	5	22,781	103.55
9,639-30	Pallet		100			3,000	2.41	241	5	18,600	84.55
8,242	Pallet	2,000	200			3,000	1.24	248	5	18,596	84.53
VT4819	Pallet	24,900	3,600	24	86,500	1,200	1.15	4,140	65	15,821	71.91
DX3813	Pallet	15,000	1,000			3,600	1.2	1,200	5	13,998	63.63
3,248-48	Pallet	200	200			4,800	2.54	508	3	12,300	55.91

expect to use in the future and pushes them to each production location in advance of use. After my earlier tirades about MRP and forecasting, there is no need to explain again why I believe the push process is a flawed model.

Working Out What to Order and Stock

In a pull system, the ordering of parts is triggered by the usage of parts in production. The most common term used to describe pull replenishment is *Kanban.*

Kanban is a Japanese term meaning "shop sign." The inspiration for *Kanban* systems was a visit to a US supermarket by Toyota Production System pioneer Taiichi Ohno. Ohno's vision was that the supply of parts to a production line could operate like replenishing shelves in a supermarket. When the line uses parts, it sends a signal to the upstream workstations, parts and raw material stores, or the supplier to replenish more of the same part. The supplier (internal or external) then supplies a prearranged quantity to the required location within a predetermined lead-time and frequency. Often, small cards are used to send the signal from the production line to the upstream processes, telling them what to supply. These are commonly called *Kanban* cards and are ubiquitous in the automotive industry where *Kanban* supply is the norm. However, there is a range of different types of pull systems used in Lean manufacturing, and *Kanban* cards are not required in all of them.

In a *Kanban* card system, a card is attached to each container of materials. As the materials are consumed on the production line, the cards are removed and returned to the upstream process or to the supplier. Parts are then picked or manufactured in the quantities specified on the *Kanban* cards. The cards are attached to the new containers, and the replacement parts sent back to the line. Usually, multiple *Kanban* cards are required for each part. To calculate the number of cards, determine the lead-time required to return the cards to the upstream process or supplier, replenish the consumed parts, and return replacement parts to the downstream process. You then need to calculate the maximum (not the average) number of parts that will be consumed by the downstream process over this replenishment lead-time. Divide this by the number of parts per container to obtain the number of *Kanban* cards you need in circulation for each part. You can then adjust (increase or decrease) the number of parts in circulation by adding or removing *Kanban* cards from the system. The challenge in using

Figure 9.2   These stillages for pressed ends and baffles for fuel tanks act as *Kanban* cards. When they are returned to the press shop empty, this is a signal for them to be replenished.

Kanban cards comes down to this: If you have a lot of parts and materials, you have a lot of cards in circulation. Because each card represents an amount of inventory, if a card gets lost, that quantity of inventory will not be replenished and that might lead to a shortage.

If you are going to rely heavily on *Kanban* cards, it pays to make an individual responsible for managing and auditing the system. TXM has helped customers set up systems using returnable containers or part stillages, where the containers take the place of the *Kanban* cards as in the example in Figure 9.2. This reduces the risk of loss because it is more difficult to lose a container than a small laminated card. The downside is that the containers (stillages) can take up a lot of space and may not even be possible if suppliers are a long distance from your factory. Suppliers may not agree to stillages if they prefer shipping parts using their own product packaging.

For small, low-value items, a two-bin system can be a simple alternative to *Kanban* cards. In a two-bin system, a maximum of two bins of parts are held at the downstream process. The bins are usually clearly labeled with the part number and quantity of parts they contain. One bin will be in use and the second bin will be full, awaiting use. When the first bin is empty, the worker drops it down a return chute or places it in a designated location

Figure 9.3 Example of a two-bin system used for electrical components. The front bin is consumed first. When it is empty, it is returned for replenishment, and the rear bin slides forward to continue supply. When the first bin is replenished, it is then loaded back in the rear rack.

for material handlers to pick up. The empty bin is then returned to the store or supplier. The quantity in each bin is calculated to allow enough time for the empty bin to be replenished before the worker runs out of parts.

Two-bin systems work well but rely on short lead-times because the parts must be replenished before the bin in use is empty. They generally work only for items that can be supplied from a store to the line, or for items where the supplier offers regular (daily or, at most, weekly) deliveries. They are commonly used for product lines such as fasteners and consumables such as the one in Figure 9.3. As the replenishment lead-time increases, it becomes necessary to introduce more bins to maintain supply and the system reverts to the multicard *Kanban* system.

Reorder Point *Kanban* Systems

A variation of the two-bin system that can avoid or delay the need for introducing multiple *Kanban* cards is the reorder point system. This system is useful when the minimum order quantity is large. For example, the paint company referred to in the case study at the end of Chapter 8 had a number of materials that could only be ordered in 200-liter drums but had low usage, so a drum might represent 3 months' worth of inventory. Therefore, if a two-bin system approach was applied, the factory would have to hold up to 6 months' worth of inventory. In this instance, the team decided to decant a small quantity (typically 20 liters) out of each drum and considered that a reorder point. When a full drum was emptied, the *Kanban* card on that drum was returned for reordering, and the factory was left with the reorder quantity (the 20-liter drum) to use until the next full drum was delivered.

This solution can work effectively in similar circumstances but it has the drawback of creating some non-value-adding work by packaging the reorder quantity. It is less effective with long lead-time operations. The reorder point must *always* be equal to or less than the quantity ordered from the supplier. Otherwise, the parts or materials delivery will not be enough to replenish the inventory to the reorder point. If the lead-time is long, or demand for the parts very variable, a large reorder point is needed to avoid running out of stock during the replenishment period. This may lead to excessive stock because the order quantity would need to be increased to match or exceed the order quantity. In this case, a better option would be to introduce multiple *Kanban* cards.

Using Computerized Min-Max Systems

Manufacturers often have an aversion to using something as simple as *Kanban* cards or a two-bin system to control materials. Surely in the twenty-first century, we should be using a computer!

Most computerized enterprise requirements planning (ERP) systems do have a built-in form of pull replenishment. These are usually min-max systems. Minimum and maximum stock levels are loaded into the ERP system for each part. At set intervals, a report highlights every item that has fallen below the minimum stock level and recommends an order quantity to bring the count back to the maximum stock level.

These are effectively computerized reorder point systems. They can be used as an alternative and potentially have the benefits (and drawbacks) of a reorder point system. The problem is that they rely on the accuracy of the inventory in the ERP system. If the inventory count is inaccurate, it may order stock when it is not needed, or run out of stock before replenishment is triggered. Also, delays between physical usage or receipt of stock and updating of virtual inventory on the ERP system can mean that inventory records are inaccurate at any point in time and min-max levels are wrong. We find that small and medium-sized enterprises (SMEs) have a difficult time maintaining accurate raw material and work-in-progress (WIP) inventory in real time due to recording delays. Therefore, it is much better to use a replenishment trigger based on physical inventory such as a *Kanban* card.

Ordering from the Supplier

In the automotive industry, it is common to send *Kanban* cards to the supplier; but in other industries where the system is not as well understood and lost *Kanban* cards are common, this may not be a good idea. Typically, *Kanban* cards will be delivered to the raw materials store or purchasing office, and an official order or requisition generated and sent to the supplier. The advantage of this approach is that from a supplier's point of view, it is business as usual; the supplier receives a purchase order and sends the specified number of parts to that purchase order. The SLA specifies lead-time and delivery frequency, and prevents the supplier from grouping *Kanban* orders together and delivering them in one shipment.

Alternatively, some companies use a fax ban. This is a pro-forma fax or e-mail that lists all the materials ordered from the supplier along with specific quantities to be supplied the next day. This form is usually filled out each day with the requirements from that supplier and faxed or e-mailed to them for supply the next day.

Assuming a company generates a new order for every *Kanban* card, this represents a huge number of orders and a lot of transactional work. To circumvent this problem, many companies create monthly blanket orders for their suppliers. These specify an approximate quantity for the month. *Kanban* orders or fax bans are recorded against this order number, and at the end of the month the order quantity is adjusted to match the actual quantity delivered. From an accounting governance point of view, the supplier needs to provide a dispatch docket or other proof of delivery for each delivery that can then be matched against their own record of what was delivered.

Key Points in Chapter 9

■ A pull system where material is pulled from upstream processes, stores, and suppliers to replace materials used in the process is the most effective and reliable system for managing materials in a factory. A push system, where materials are pushed to a location in advance of use based on a forecast, is less effective due to the limitations of forecasting and often lead to excess inventory and shortages.

■ *Kanban* is a form of pull system where returnable cards or containers are used to represent a set amount of inventory. Return of the *Kanban* to the supplier is the trigger for supplying the exact quantity of material back to the process. Materials are only supplied when a *Kanban* is returned empty.

■ Any system for controlling material requires a level of shop-floor discipline, and the systems described above are no exception. If products are not returned to their correct location or *Kanban* cards and product bins get lost, then the system quickly breaks down.

■ To create this level of shop-floor control, we frequently implement 5S techniques (see Chapter 11) to *create a discipline of a place for everything and everything in its place.*

■ The role of the front-line supervisor is also critical in ensuring that the system is maintained and improved. In our experience, the effort is worth it. *Shortages are typically reduced by more than 90%, customer lead-times are cut in half, and inventory is reduced by 50%.* The levels of expediting and stress are also dramatically reduced, thereby saving management time and improving relationships with suppliers, who then view their customer (you) as well organized and predictable. For suppliers, that translates to lower costs—a savings they will hopefully share with you.

Reference

1. Harris, R., Harris, C., and Wilson, E. 2003. *Making Materials Flow: A Lean Material-Handling Guide for Operations, Production-Control, and Engineering Professionals.* Cambridge, MA: Lean Enterprise Institute.

Chapter 10

Developing Your Team

What You Will Learn in This Chapter

- Lean leadership behaviors to help you get the best out of your front-line teams
- Visual management: how to engage your teams in improving factory performance every day
- Lean daily leadership: creating daily routines for yourself and your leaders that will drive ongoing performance
- Using A3 plans to communicate strategy and major projects

Can You Become a "Lean Leader"?

We now have all the elements of a production system for a successful small or medium-sized factory in place, so how do we now lead this operation? We hear a lot about leadership. Hundreds of books, seminars, and experts tell you how you should be a better leader. The theme of Lean conferences in the past few years has been all about "Lean leadership." I am often bemused by the Lean leadership discussion, as I think it self-evident that clear leadership is essential to the success of Lean just as it is to every major change or initiative that your business is attempting. In short, if the boss does not support it, it is not going to happen.

So what is special about a Lean leader, and how do you become a Lean leader? First, you cannot change who you are as a person—your underlying values, your personality. A lot of managers attempt this and come across as unconvincing or, worse, untrustworthy. So you cannot change *who you are*, but you can change *what you do*. That is, you can change your behavior and habits. We all have habits—automatic behaviors that we demonstrate without thinking, meaning they are often driven by our subconscious rather than conscious thinking. We can change habits but it takes discipline. The key to being a successful leader—and particularly a successful Lean leader—is to demonstrate positive leadership habits.

So what are the habits you need?

Regularly Spend Time on the Shop Floor

This is not just going for a walk and a chat "once in a blue moon." Value is created on the factory floor, and therefore manufacturing leaders (and leaders in any industry) need to spend time regularly with their front-line employees. This means taking time to observe the process and providing constructive feedback on what you observe. Write your observations in a notebook. Follow a regular route around your factory. The aim is not to ambush your teams or to catch them at idle moments, but rather to show them you are interested and engaged in what they are doing. When I worked as the plant manager in a plastics molding plant, I had a checklist of things in my notebook that I would aim to observe every day. The kinds of questions I wanted to find the answers to included

- What problems did the production teams have, and were their leaders supporting them to resolve those problems?
- What was in the waste bin? Were we throwing out good product? What kinds of defects were prevalent?
- Was the manning level correct, and were the team members following standard work?
- What was the quality of finished goods?
- Were production machines running according to predetermined cycles?
- Was automated inspection equipment switched on and working correctly?
- What was occupying the time of team leaders and managers?

I am sure that you will find a lot of other things to add to your checklist that are relevant to your factory. Do not aim to check on everything, and do not try to check every item on your list every day. You should also review your checklist and add new items as problems arise and remove them when you consistently find that performance is good. This shows that you are actually engaged in the process, rather than just being bureaucratic. These kinds of questions and observations will demonstrate your involvement and will let the team know current priorities.

Armed with your observations, you can engage in discussion with shop-floor leaders. *These must be focused on asking why things are not as they should be or, equally, asking why things are going so well.*

Avoid accusations or judgments. For example, if you march up to a supervisor and say, for example, "The amount of waste in the bin is unacceptable! Who made all this rubbish?", you will get a defensive response and are also likely to get a lot of finger-pointing and few answers. Instead, if you open the conversation with "I notice there are a lot of these moldings in the bin. Are you having problems with that part?", then you open up a problem-solving discussion. You always need to ask "Why?" to help your team members explain the root causes of the problem, avoiding any compulsion you might have to tell employees the solution. You also need to ask about good performance and how employees achieved it. For example, "I notice that we haven't made any defects so far this shift. How have we achieved this?" This gives the team leader a chance to tell his success story, and helps you learn about him and about your process. It will have far more impact than simply saying "Well done."

Beyond your checklist you need to keep your eyes open as you walk around. The purpose of visual controls and visual management (see Chapter 11) is to visualize the status of production and highlight any abnormalities. However, this is only effective if leaders notice those abnormalities. For example, if you walk past and ignore an overflowing first-in-first-out (FIFO) lane, equipment not in the correct location, a large stock of defective products, or empty *Kanban* locations, then you are sending a message to your employees that these issues are not important. People will respond to what you see as important. By ignoring nonstandard work or procedures (passive acceptance), you will fatally undermine your production system. You set the example.*

As you will have determined by now, a proper visit to the shop floor takes time. It is not just a 5-minute walk-through on the way to the next meeting. *The value we create for customers is created in our factories.*

---

* For simple ideas on how to approach these conversations, view our Lean Minute Video: *The Toyota Method of Respecting People.* http://txm.com.au/video/txm-lean-minute-video-toyota-method-respecting-people

Therefore, an hour per day observing how that value is being created and providing feedback to the employees creating it would seem like a good investment of a manufacturing manager's time.

Ask Why Five Times

As leaders and managers we often interpret our role as one to direct and control. In the seminal *Harvard Business Review* article titled "Learning to Lead at Toyota,"[1] Spear explains that at Toyota, leaders see their roles as coaches, teaching their teams to observe and experiment to improve the process. To do this means focusing on asking questions rather than giving orders. However, when you ask why, be prepared to go beyond the obvious superficial answer, such as "The worker made a mistake," to get to the root cause of the problem. By doing this, you learn the real opportunities in your business; but more importantly, you teach your team members to go beyond the obvious and look for the root cause of problems. There is further discussion on the importance of problem solving in Chapter 11.*

Keeping Track of Performance: Visual Management

You need to ensure that teams see your interest in everyday performance, but the teams also need to take accountability for their own everyday performance. This is often best done using visual management. Again, there are many books written on visual management, so the aim here is just to provide some key concepts.

In Chapter 7 we worked out the key measures for your business. However, having these metrics confined to a computer or in a monthly report distributed among managers is not really going to drive improvement. Every team at every level of your organization needs its own scoreboard, or visual management board. We usually get teams to set up a whiteboard (typically 900 mm × 1,200 mm or larger) in a prominent location in their workspace, such as the one in Figure 10.1. The location should be easily accessible and away from forklift traffic and excessive noise because it is the location in which the team will have their daily meetings.

---

* To learn more about how to ask "why," view our TXM Lean Minute Video: *Ask Why Five Times.* http://txm.com.au/video/txm-lean-minute-video-ask-five-times

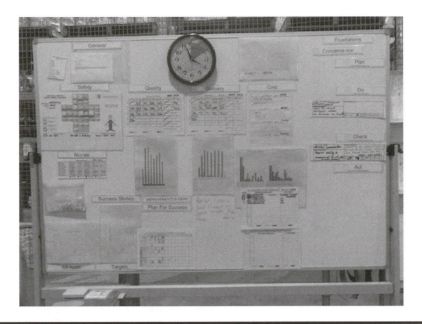

Figure 10.1 Example visual management board for a TXM customer. The clock in the center shows the daily meeting time.

Typically we separate the visual management board into broad subject categories. You can choose your own but our customers often choose production, delivery, quality, safety, and morale. Try to limit yourself to one or a maximum of two metrics per category. Big boards with too many metrics only lead to confusion. In fact, to get started in a business where teams are not accustomed to measuring performance, it can be a good idea to start with just one metric (such as daily output in units) and then gradually add other metrics as the team grows in confidence and wants to understand the drivers of daily output.

Maintenance of an up-to-date visual management board is the responsibility of the team leader (or manager) in charge of the area. *Do not* allow this task to be outsourced to an external department because it is important that the team takes responsibility for updating its own metrics in its own work area. To this end, we recommend the use of handwritten graphs rather than having them printed on a computer in an office. The metrics can be updated live during the daily team meeting (see below) and provide points of discussion. Highlighting target performance in green and off-target performance in red can also drive home the meaning of the numbers much more effectively than just printing out an Excel® graph on a printer.

Some businesses like highly standardized visual boards to give a "corporate look." Standardizing the look of the visual boards is not important. What matters is that the team has ownership of the board and the metrics on it, and considers it as their own and a key tool for getting feedback about their daily (or hourly) performance.

Meet Daily

In my experience as a manufacturing leader, I found that there was no substitute for regular structured communication with your team. You can have a dozen informal water-cooler conversations but until you get the team together and discuss things as a group, they are unlikely to feel properly consulted and involved in decision making. We recommend that every leader meet with his or her team every day. This provides an opportunity to review performance, plan for the next day, and solve problems. This meeting must be structured with an agenda, occur at the same time each day, and take no longer than 10 minutes. We usually suggest that this meeting occurs standing up, with the team clustered around a visual management board such as the one shown in Figure 10.2.

Figure 10.2 Daily meeting under way at the visual management board in a TXM customer's factory.

Start the meeting by updating the key metrics on the board and discussing the previous day's performance. Begin with safety and then move on to production, quality, and other issues of the day. Cover the highlights of both good and substandard performance. Do not get into too much detail. Issues can be highlighted for simple problem solving. Discuss what is happening on the current day, along with any company news or announcements; then throw the floor open for team members to raise problems. These can be dealt with using simple structured problem-solving techniques such as Five Whys.* If you are the leader, then make sure that you ask questions and focus on why rather than make accusations and focus on individuals. Keep the tone positive—poor performance is an opportunity to improve, and problems are an opportunity to learn and strengthen your processes.

If you are visiting the meeting as a manager, do not take over. Let the team leader run it, and *never* correct him or her in front of the team. Focus on observing and asking questions at the end, unless you have particular news to impart. *It is vital for the team to see that you respect the role of their team leader. If you need to give feedback to the team leader about his team or the running of the meeting, give it to him in private, one on one after the meeting.*

Many team leaders may be reluctant to run a team meeting in front of their team. Therefore, you will need to coach them. This coaching may start with you leading the first few meetings and then observing and providing feedback until the new team leader is leading the discussion with confidence. If the individual is completely unwilling to lead the team meeting, that person most likely is the wrong person to lead the team, and another individual should be selected.

Daily meetings should form a routine. Figure 10.3 shows a typical day in the life of a production team. Team leaders hold their daily meetings with their teams at the start of the shift at 7:10 a.m. after they have updated their team board. At midmorning (perhaps after the morning break), the manufacturing manager does his daily shop-floor walk. Throughout the morning, production planning updates the schedule and plans the following day's production. After lunch, the team leaders and manufacturing manager meet with planning and procurement to plan the next day's production and share information that affects the schedule. At the end of the shift or day,

---

* An incisive problem-solving technique used to identify root causes for problems.

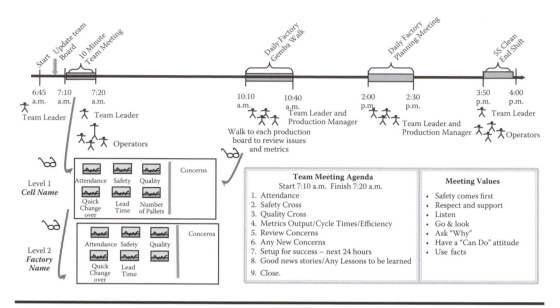

Figure 10.3 A "day in the life" of team leaders in a Lean factory.

the teams take 5 to 10 minutes to do routine housekeeping tasks. Figure 10.3 shows the routine on a daily timeline.

Planning on a Page: The A3 Plan

We can drown in information. Reports, presentations, and e-mails load every manager with a massive amount of information to read and digest every day. So how do you get and then communicate the information that is really important? Toyota uses a simple tool called the A3 plan. This is exactly what it sounds like: a plan or initiative explained on a single, A3-sized piece of paper. There are excellent books available on A3 planning and the Toyota system for deploying strategy, otherwise called *hoshin* planning. Two of the best are *Managing to Learn* by Shook[2] and, my favorite, *Getting the Right Things Done* by Dennis.[3]

A3 plans are used to communicate a wide range of messages. They can be used for problem solving, communicating strategy, and developing improvement plans, and to describe action plans and their timetables, present major initiatives, and report on business progress and performance. I think a huge amount of time and paper could be saved if companies insisted that monthly reports be limited to a single, A3-sized piece of paper.

The key elements of an A3 plan include

1. The entire plan should take up no more than a single side of one A3-sized piece of paper. (And this should not be achieved by using tiny fonts!)
2. The A3 plan should tell a story. Typically, a series of textboxes and diagrams should define the issue, outline the current state, describe the future state, and lay out the steps and resources required to achieve the future state.
3. The use of bold type for key points should provide a very brief overview of the plan. In other words, reading just the bold type will provide a general idea of what is being communicated.

To deploy business strategy, A3 plans are generally cascaded through an organization. The operations A3 plan is developed after the overall business plan A3 and reflects the operations department's contribution to the overall strategic goals outlined in the business plan. Likewise, the A3 plan for the warehouse is developed after the operations plan and shows how the warehouse supports achieving the operations plan. In this way, functions and levels are aligned in making their contribution to the achievement of the overall strategy. Ultimately, the A3 planning process can be extended down to the individual team level so that each team leader has an A3 plan for his or her area.

A key theme of this chapter has been the need to lead by example. For the use of A3 plans to be effective, you, the leader, should use them to communicate, and insist that initiatives and plans communicated to you are presented in that same way.

Key Points in Chapter 10

■ As discussed at the start of this chapter, there are an untold number of books on leadership; in writing this book, I have made a conscious decision not to add to the list. I am aware that many of my Lean colleagues will no doubt criticize me for dedicating only one chapter to leadership. For those readers interested in learning more, my suggestion is that you read some of the published books dedicated to Lean leadership.

■ You need to ensure that your messages and approach to management are consistent over time. The key to forming and maintaining good leadership habits is repetition, so that they become a natural way of doing things. This repetition creates trust with your team as they know how you are likely to behave, the focus of your efforts, and how you achieve your goals. Your example sets the way.

■ Create a daily routine where you visit the factory floor and observe how value is being created for your customers.

■ A simple checklist can help you focus on the important things as you walk around.

■ Try to ask questions of your people rather than giving orders or making criticisms.

■ Encourage your teams to measure their performance and display their measures on a visual management board in their workplace.

■ Recognize that problems are opportunities to improve and when things go wrong, ask why five times, not "who?"

■ Create routine daily communication where team leaders have short daily "standup" meetings with their teams and then meet once a day with yourself to plan the next few days' production.

■ Use A3 one page plans to communicate strategy or projects.

■ Remember that your people follow your example, so watch your behaviors and be consistent.

References

1. Spear, S.J. Learning to Lead at Toyota, *Harvard Business Review*, May 2004. http://hbr.org/2004/05/learning-to-lead-at-toyota/ar/1
2. Shook, J. 2008. *Managing to Learn: Using the A3 Management Process to Solve Problems, Gain Agreement, Mentor and Lead.* Cambridge, MA: Lean Enterprise Institute.
3. Dennis, P. 2006. *Getting the Right Things Done: A Leader's Guide to Planning and Execution.* Cambridge, MA: Lean Enterprise Institute.

Chapter 11

Locking in the Gains: The Need for Standardization

What You Will Learn in This Chapter

- What is standard work, how it differs from "time and motion studies," and why you need it in your business
- How to develop standard work
- How to create a visual workplace using 5S
- How to use simple root cause analysis and problem-solving techniques every day to improve performance

What Is Standard Work?

Chapter 2 introduced Spear and Bowen's four rules of the Toyota Production System. Rule 1: *All work is standardized in terms of content, sequence, timing, and outcome.*[1] Standardization is the foundation of Lean manufacturing. The first questions a Toyota Lean specialist asks when faced with a problem are, "What is the standard?" and "Did we follow the standard?"

However, for most of the small and medium-sized enterprise (SME) manufacturers described in this book, work is not standardized; it is mostly defined in terms of outcome, although this can often be ambiguous (for example, accepting borderline-quality work). It may have some definition in terms of content (what is the job?), but it is highly unlikely to be defined in terms of operational sequence and timing. The result is that it is left to each worker to define what he does, what order he does it in, and how long the operation takes. This might seem like a Lean approach because it puts the worker in control and lets him design his own work, but there are huge problems with this nonstandardized approach, including

- Every worker will do the task differently, with different steps in a different order, taking a different length of time, and delivering a different outcome. The result is variable quality and variable production rates.
- When things go wrong, it is almost impossible to define root causes, and the workers are inevitably blamed.
- The process often builds in large amounts of waste because the worker is expected to figure out how to get the job done, but he is generally not empowered to change the tools he is provided, the layout of the workplace, or the location of materials.
- If the work has not been standardized for timing and the time taken to complete the work varies from worker to worker, it is likely that there will be large imbalances between processes.

In our experience, the impact of this lack of standard work on productivity is enormous. Typically we increase labor productivity 40% to 50% by implementing the process outlined below. Quality improvements can also be dramatic with reductions in internal rework and scrap in particular often in excess of 90%.

Standard Work, Industrial Engineering, and Scientific Management

Around the turn of the twentieth century, an American named Fredrick Taylor did a series of studies on steelworkers. He observed that much of their effort was unproductive, resulting in the seven wastes outlined in Chapter 2. Workers lost time due to unnecessary movement and walking, the absence of simple tools and jigs, and the lack of structure in their work. Taylor deduced that a scientific approach could be applied to designing work so that workers performed tasks the same way each time in clearly defined sequences with a resulting increase in productivity. Part of his design included methods to eliminate unnecessary work that burdened workers. He called the result "scientific management." The most famous follower of Taylor's thinking was Henry Ford, who combined the "killing chain" methodology he had seen for processing cattle in a slaughterhouse with Taylor's scientific approach to job design, thereby creating the first moving production line assembling Ford's Model T. Ford's assembly line dramatically reduced the cost of building a car and, combined with a simple robust design, enabled him to transform the automotive industry by putting motoring within reach of ordinary people.

The problem was that Taylor's approach tended to treat the worker like a machine. Industrial engineers observed and recorded workers' movements, and using a range of labor tables and standards, planned the job the worker was required to follow. I suspect that Taylor's concern for reducing unnecessary burden on the worker was quickly forgotten in the rush to increase output and profits. But workers are not machines and do not appreciate being treated as such. The scientific management approach led to increasing worker alienation and frustration, which provided fertile ground for radical union leaders and rampant unionization, especially in the English-speaking world.

Almost anyone who has completed a business degree will have heard this story, and Taylor's scientific management approach is now almost universally discredited in management schools around the world. However, this dismissal of Taylor does him and his work a disservice, as he profoundly influenced manufacturing thinking around the world, and his thinking is the basis of Lean standardized work. However, standardized work is not scientific management, and it is important to understand the differences.

In my opinion, the basis of standard work comes from the different work culture that existed in Japan and Germany, as opposed to that in the English-speaking world. In Japan and Germany, work has always been a collaborative endeavor where workers, management, and unions work together for the betterment of the company and the nation. Unions and workers are often represented on management boards, and employees usually have exceptional job security and are highly respected for (and very proud of) their skills and professionalism. In this environment, it would have been quite alien for management to develop standard work procedures without involving and consulting the workers who did the work. Instead, work standards were developed with the teams and therefore they had a strong say regarding how work was done. In English-speaking countries, managers, with some justification, given the confrontational nature of many workplaces, did not trust workers to design their own work. In postwar Germany and Japan, the mutual respect and sense of common purpose that existed in large organizations such as Toyota and Volkswagen meant that workers were involved in setting the standards.

The purpose of this lengthy discussion is to make it clear that to be successful, standard work must be developed at the team level, ideally by the team on the factory floor with the support of industrial engineers, designers, and other management functions as required. *It should never be a top-down process.* Managers should never forget that they do not perform the work—the workers do. *The greatest expert on any job will be the person who has been performing that job for years. The purpose of standard work is to extract and document that knowledge.*

As Lean coaches, we aim to find the best way for team members from all appropriate levels of the manufacturing organization to work together to identify any techniques or tricks of the trade, and identify and eliminate sources of waste such as poor work cell design or inadequate tools and fixtures. The first step in achieving standardized work is to standardize how things in the workplace are organized. The tool we use to do this is called 5S.

The First Step toward Standard Work: 5S and the Visual Workplace

When you work in an office, you are usually provided with your own office or cubicle. Within certain guidelines, you are free to arrange how your cubicle or office is laid out to best suit your needs. You can decide what pictures to hang, what books you need, where to put the phone or computer on your desk, and, in most cases, where to place your desk and furniture.

In contrast, when you first start employment as a worker in a factory, the process is totally different. You are shown your workplace, you are given your tools (or told what to buy), you are told the location of materials, and you begin working. You are likely to have no say regarding your workplace arrangement, and the fact that you have to walk 40 steps to move a part from one process to the next process 100 times a day is something you will put up with for years or even decades because that is the way the workplace is arranged and you are not empowered to change it. 5S is a system that empowers workers to change their workplace. It is also the first step toward engaging workers in developing standard work. The elements of 5S are

- Sorting what is in the area to determine what is needed, what can be stored elsewhere, and what can be disposed of.
- Setting in order the area by determining a place for everything and putting everything in its place.
- Making the area shine by giving it a thorough cleaning from top to bottom in order to set a new benchmark for housekeeping and cleanliness and (frequently) to reveal the sources of dirt.
- Standardizing the workplace by establishing standards and procedures to constantly maintain the standard of the area. This can include checklists, simple tools to track regular cleaning tasks, and setting clear roles and responsibilities. This is then locked in by
- Sustaining the change by implementing ongoing improvements and audit results. This establishes a culture of continually increasing production, cutting costs, improving quality, cutting waste, and improving safety methods.

Once again, there are lots of books on 5S. If you want a quick introduction, start with *5S for Operators: 5 Pillars of the Visual Workplace* by Hirano et al.[2] If you have more time and more enthusiasm, the "seminal text" on 5S is *5 Pillars of the Visual Workplace* by Hirano.[3]

Getting started on 5S is straightforward:

- Choose a pilot area somewhere highly visible within your workplace.
- Designate an area where you can temporarily store items that you remove from the pilot area and also a red tag area to hold items that the team has not decided whether to use or how and where to use them.
- Arrange a time when you can gather the workers in that area and, particularly the team leaders off the clock, for about 4 hours.
- After providing them with a quick introduction to 5S principles, have the team remove everything from the area that is not bolted down.
- They next should sort the things (tools, fixtures, jigs, pallets, etc.) that are used every day, things that are used regularly (e.g., every week), things that are used infrequently (e.g., once a month or less), implements that are very rarely or never used, and things that should be discarded.
- The team then decides the placement of the things they need in their area. Items used all the time are placed in highly accessible places, while implements used less frequently may be placed in less-convenient

locations or kept outside the work cell to be brought in when needed. Items that are rarely or never used might be given red tags and placed in the red tag area where they can be stored until a final decision is made on whether they can be disposed of.

■ The team then thoroughly cleans the workplace, removing all layers of dirt on floors, walls, and machinery. In the process, they might find maintenance issues such as oil or air leaks or broken guards. They should tag and record these items for maintenance to fix.

■ Next they draw lines to locate the things in the pilot area, set up shelves and other containers, ensure that the places they have selected for things are clearly identified, and perform other incidental tasks that help in making the pilot area effective.

■ Finally, they establish visual controls, such as the shadow board displayed in Figure 11.1, which contains the tools and standardized instructions for controlling the workplace operation.

Once the team has completed this setup, their workplace looks radically better. The question then becomes how to keep it that way.

Here's how: The first thing is to take a photograph, laminate it, and post it on the wall in a visible location in the work area. This becomes the

Figure 11.1   Example of 5S visual controls at a TXM customer.

5S Standard Packing

Sort Out
- Floor clear
- No excess items

Set In Order
- Broom & Shovel in place
- Shovel facing inward
- Walkway clear

Shine & Check
- Swept daily
- Wipe fence monthly

Standardize
- Standard displayed
- Shared zone defined

Sustain
- One improvement in Packing Area/month

Figure 11.2   Example of a visual standard of a TXM customer.

standard, showing how the workplace should look; see Figure 11.2. Team members may also want to add some comments on what they expect to see when others visit the workplace.

The final step is to establish an audit process to sustain and continuously improve 5S performance. This involves reviewing each work area and comparing it to the visual standard. We recommend conducting weekly 5S audits. We also think that team leaders should audit their own areas. The argument often given is that team leaders may give themselves a good audit score when their area does not deserve it. We feel this argument misses the point. The audit score is only an indicator of improvement. It will never be objective, and the real judge of performance is visible for everyone to see: Does the area match the visual standard on the wall, and is it improving? The benefit of team leaders doing their own audit is that they are more likely to get it done because they have a greater stake in their own work area than anyone else, and it also requires them to analyze and take responsibility for their own area.

Moving from 5S to Standard Work

The reason why 5S is such a great place to start is that it engages front-line employees in organizing their own workspaces, and then sets a standard for organization that all employees agree to follow, maintain, and improve.

When talking about how the workplace should be arranged, the conversation inevitably turns to what work is done in the workplace and how it is done. This is the starting point for a conversation on standardized work.

In Chapter 4 we defined a *takt* time for your process: the production rate needed to keep up with the average rate at which customers are buying your product. This *takt* time measurement is the yardstick by which we will measure the work in our process.

The first step in developing standard work is to get workers to write down what they actually do. It starts with a simple list of all the steps involved to complete one worker's specific task. Ask all workers who carry out this task to complete their own list of tasks and compare those lists among the team. Alternatively you can ask the most competent worker to complete a list and then share this with the others for their feedback. If you can agree among the workers on the best order in which to do the tasks at this point, do so; otherwise, use the next stage to gather data on a range of alternative approaches so you can compare them objectively.

The next step is timing the process. This should be handled with sensitivity as few enjoy being timed. It can work best when the team leader and team members work together to do the timing. Make sure they time several cycles from the same work being done by several different workers. Highlight walking time and machine cycle times involved in the work. It can also be interesting to separate value-added and non-value-added time (using the seven wastes highlighted in Chapter 2). Also note any tips and techniques that workers have developed to simplify the tasks or achieve better outcomes. From the various combinations they will find the optimum sequence of tasks and a standard time in which an average worker can perform each task consistently. (*Note:* Avoid setting the standard based on the fastest or slowest worker.)

To get a visual understanding of the process, a spaghetti diagram is useful, such as the one in Figure 11.3. It shows the path and distance moved by the worker in completing all the process steps. This enables the team to calculate the amount of walking time involved in a process and often helps them identify simple solutions to reduce movement and waste. Typically, we assume that each step is around 75 cm long and takes approximately 1 second. Those standard measurements can help the team calculate the walking times in their processes.

The team now has a list of all the process steps and how long they take. Next they should arrange these to balance the workload across the team's

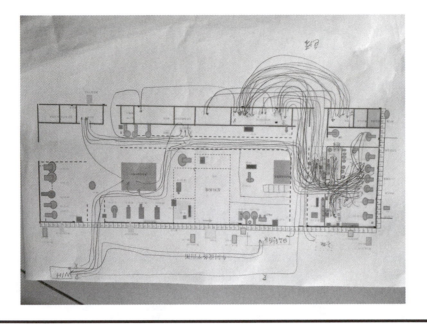

Figure 11.3 Example spaghetti diagram showing the movement of people and materials in a plant.

operations. We typically use a simple bar chart called a line balance chart to make sure that the work is leveled as much as possible across all workstations, and that each worker can complete his or her task within the *takt* time. The use of sticky notes can aid in the creation of a line balance chart by a team, such as in Figure 11.4.

The final step is to document, in a standardized worksheet, the tasks the team has designed. This worksheet displays the sequence of process steps, standard times, layout, and movement of the worker during the work cycle, and notes any critical points such as hazards, quality checks, or tasks requiring particular skills or techniques. Figure 11.5 shows a completed standardized worksheet. From this standard worksheet, training procedures (job instructions) are developed, and employees are trained in these tasks.

As explained at the start of this chapter, successful standardized work must be developed with your team, and it becomes the responsibility of the team leaders to own the standards, record any updates, and ensure that their team can work to a standard. You achieve this by developing the standards with the team leader and his or her team, and by showing respect for their contributions.

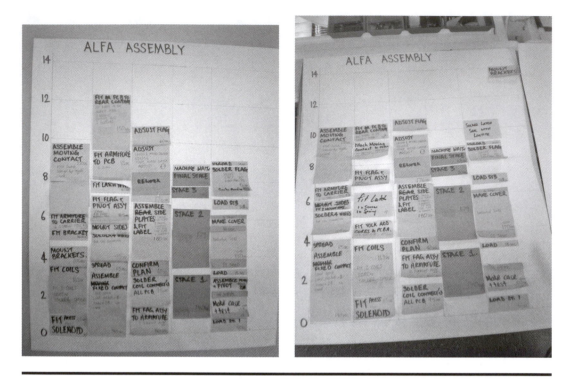

Figure 11.4   Example line balance chart. The chart on the left shows the tasks before leveling, and the chart on the right shows the tasks after leveling. *Takt* **time in this case was 10 minutes.**

When Things Go Wrong: Solving Problems Every Day

When you start measuring factory performance daily or hourly, and ensure that workers are performing according to standards, improvements are likely. However, those improvements are likely to be temporary unless you address some of the underlying performance drivers.

Every day, little things go wrong in a manufacturing business. It might be changes in raw material quality, shortages, machine breakdowns, a new worker who has not been adequately trained, or an inaccurate part drawing. Our typical behavior is to fix the symptom in front of us, to find some material, patch the machine, sort out the defects, and get the process going again; and then to declare victory and move on to the next problem. We call this approach "firefighting" and it tends to lock in the cost of risk of poor quality. That is, we expect things to go wrong and reward the troubleshooters who find temporary solutions.

Chapter 2 discussed the need to solve problems using the scientific method. Problem solving is the subject of many books (and perhaps a TXM

Jsf Controlled Environment Standard Worksheet

Site:		Std Work Sheet No:			Date:		Page:		Takt Time:					

Department Name: | | | | Process Description: |

					Time Observations			
Step No.	WORK STEPS	Component	Machine	Key	Man.	Auto	Walk	
1	Honing Rough & Finish	Sleeve	MBC1803		0.5			
2	Honing - Polishing	Sleeve	ML5000		5		1	
3	Center Grind	Slide	Technica		2	3		
4	OD and Shoulder Grinding	Sleeve	S40 - 2		2	18	1	
5	Unload and Inspect Rough Turning	Sleeve	MBC1803		3			
6	Unload finished part and load rough part	Sleeve	ML5000		3			
7	Clean finished sleeve in White Spirits	Sleeve	White Spirits		3		2	
8	Clean in Ultrasonic Tank	Sleeve	Ultrasonic		2	7		
9	Final bore inspection	Sleeve	Air Gauging		2	15	0.5	
10	Unload Ground Sleeve	Sleeve	S40 - 2		8			
11	Load slide for matching and sh'lder grind	Sleeve & Slide	S21		2	5		
12	Final Matching Inspection	Sleeve & Slide	Air Gauging		10		1	
13	Engraving	Sleeve	Engraver		2	7		
14	Grind head height	Sleeve	Mitsui		2	10		
15	Critical Part Inspection	Assembly	Talyrond	Q	15	10	3	
			Totals		61.5	75	8.5	

KEY: Safety | Quality Check | Delta Critical | In-Process Stock

Figure 11.5 Example of a standard worksheet.

book before long). However, solving problems using the scientific method means that we

- *Plan:* Analyze the problem, identify the root cause, and agree to a permanent solution.
- *Do:* Implement the agreed-upon solution.
- *Check* the results: Ensure that the solution works and the problem does not recur.
- *Act:* Lock in the solution by making it part of our standard work, our bills of materials, or our quality system.

This Plan–Do–Check–Act (PDCA) approach must permeate throughout every level of your organization, so that for every problem your teams encounter, they gain more in-depth knowledge about their processes and initiate improvements that truly eliminate recurring problems.

There are a multitude of root cause analysis tools but our favorite is a simple one, called Five Whys (discussed briefly in Chapter 10). In its most basic form, this process starts by defining the problem: What has gone wrong? You then ask why the problem has occurred until you drive to its root cause.

A typical Five Whys discussion among team members might center around the following questions and answers, the aim of which is to drill down until the team exposes the root cause of any given problem. In this case, I have described a typical plastics injection molding scenario:

Q: Why are we running slower than the standard cycle?
A: Because we were getting too much part distortion.
Q: Why were we getting too much part distortion?
A: Because the parts were too hot coming out of the mold.
Q: Why are the parts too hot coming out of the mold?
A: Because we are not getting enough cooling into the mold.
Q: Why are we not getting enough cooling into the mold?

There may be a range of causes here that we can check, such as the cooling water temperature and flow rate; but on this occasion, let's say that the answer was

A: The cooling channels in the mold are blocked.

The indicated remedial action is to schedule the mold for maintenance as soon as possible to clean out the cooling channels.

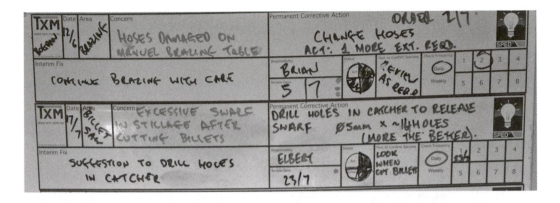

Figure 11.6 Examples of problem-solving concern strips in a machining operation.

The process does not end there. The team leader records his problem-solving activities on a magnetic "concern strip," which is a simple template for PDCA problem solving on the factory floor, and places the concern strip on his visual management board (see Figure 11.6).

When action has been taken to resolve the problem, the team leader reviews the concern strip at his daily team meeting to ensure that the problem has not recurred. Normally this check is repeated for a few days, a few production runs, or a few weeks to make sure that the problem has truly disappeared.

For many such problems, a preventive maintenance task is assigned. In the PDCA example described above, maintenance cleaned and checked that the cooling channels were done regularly. The concern strip was then closed.

In our experience, repeated use of problem solving is perhaps the greatest driver of ongoing improvement in business. It is also a process that takes the most discipline to instill in employees. It is much quicker to firefight problems, but the problem with firefighting is that the fires always come back.

Key Points in Chapter 11

- SME manufacturers typically do not standardize the work in their processes, meaning that every worker is likely to do a given job differently, take a different time, and get a slightly different outcome.
- If you do not have standards when problems arise, you have no way of knowing if the correct procedure was followed and why the problem occurred, and then it is normal to just blame the worker. Standardization helps prevent this.

■ Standard work should be developed together with teams and should be the responsibility of team leaders in your organization. A top-down approach to designing work will lead to alienation. The employees who do the work are the employees intimately familiar with the process and its problems, and are in the best position to resolve problems with your help.

■ The first step toward standard work is 5S. This powerful technique will give you a clean and organized workplace. Most importantly, it sets a standard for how work is done.

■ It is relatively easy to build standard output once you have established 5S.

■ Standard work is a team-supported process for completing a task that specifies the steps involved, the sequence they need to be completed in, how long they will take, and the expected outcomes.

■ A spaghetti diagram enables you to visualize standard work and eliminate excess movement and waste.

■ It is important to level standard work to make sure that work can be completed within the *takt* time and that processes are balanced. A Yamazumi or line balance chart* will help you see imbalances and rebalance the work.

■ There are lots of things that might prevent workers from meeting their standard work requirements. Typically, SMEs focus on fixing the symptoms of these problems so that work can continue; we call this firefighting.

■ The PDCA daily problem-solving method using concern strips employs simple root cause analysis to expose the root causes of problems, develop permanent fixes, implement those fixes, and check that the problems have been permanently resolved and the solutions locked in. Continued use of problem-solving methods is an integral component of ongoing improvements.

References

1. Spear, S. and Bowen, H.K. Decoding the DNA of the Toyota Production System. *Harvard Business Review* 77(5) 96–106, 1999.
2. Hirano H. et al. 1996. *5S for Operators: 5 Pillars of the Visual Workplace.* Portland, OR: Productivity Press.
3. Hirano, H. 1995. *5 Pillars of the Visual Workplace: The Sourcebook for 5S Implementation.* Portland, OR: Productivity Press.

---

* A stacked bar chart that reveals workload differences among workers, usually on an assembly line.

Chapter 12

Resourcing the Change

What You Will Learn in This Chapter

- What to expect when you start to make changes in your business; why it is so difficult at the beginning and why it will get easier if you persist
- The importance of properly resourcing your Lean transformation
- How to select a Lean consultant (yes, you *will* need one)
- The best approach to developing internal Lean expertise within your business
- Where to get further help

Making a Start

As discussed in Chapter 1, a characteristic of small and medium-sized manufacturers is their lack of resources compared to their big-business colleagues. In small and medium-sized enterprises (SMEs), managers have many roles and traditionally are very busy people.

After reading this book, you may come to the realization that transforming your business is going to take a lot of work. In this, you would be correct. You would also be correct if you concluded that all the problems demanding your attention will not go away while you try to improve your business. At the start of any improvement program, your workload will most certainly include all the many day-to-day problems you have to address: the late deliveries, the quality problems, the machine breakdowns, and the material shortages, to name just a few. As a result, the workload and the strain on your business will actually increase as you try to implement improvements.

Add to that the shock of change and its effect on your organization, and now you are beginning to realize the extent of the challenge facing you. Many of your planned changes are going to seem a bit strange at first and may not work perfectly. We compare it to learning a new golf swing. When the pro explains how to hold the club and swing it, the grip, stance, and swing feel foreign and uncomfortable. The temptation will be to go back to your old bad habits and keep hitting balls into the rough. However, with practice, the new swing gets better, you start hitting more balls straight down the fairway, and your new swing becomes habit.

Manufacturing improvement is like that. At first, the extra workload and the fact that the changes (such as introducing a pull system) seem strange mean that you may want nothing more than to yield to the temptation to give up. But giving up means that you go back to all the problems and fire-fighting stress you have always faced. It also means that your business won't grow, and may in fact decline and fail. Some companies look to a software fix, praying that a new enterprise requirements planning (ERP) system will provide a panacea to their problems. It will not, as explained in previous chapters. *There is no substitute for the hard work of change, and the results are worth every bit of the—to paraphrase Churchill—blood, sweat, and tears.*

But do not despair. The good news is that things get easier. Eventually, the new processes you have developed take hold, and some of the daily fires you have been so busy combating, disappear. Your new shop-floor coaching style and your team leaders' daily leadership routines will mean increasingly that problems will be resolved before you even have to deal with them. Standardization produces more consistent results and, when things go wrong, the causes are easier to spot and fix. Figure 12.1 depicts what we see as the typical pattern of improvement.

Note in Figure 12.1 that there is no scale on either axis. This is deliberate. It is impossible to say how much the total workload will increase or how long it will take before improvements take hold and start making life easier. In our experience, this depends on your level of commitment, how much improving you have to do (how poor the state of your factory is before you start), and what resources you commit to the improvement effort.

Getting Help

It is possible to follow the instructions in this book, perhaps read a number of the other recommended books, and lead the change yourself. In fact, this

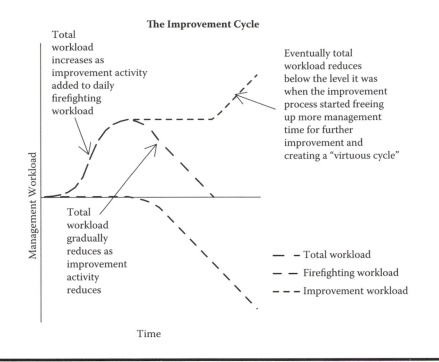

Figure 12.1   Improvement cycle charted.

was the way I was forced to implement change in my time as a manufacturing manager. This approach can be successful but it is slow, and you are likely to suffer costly mistakes and reversals along the way.

Many companies in this situation recruit a manufacturing manager with some Lean experience and expect that he or she will drive the improvement. This may be successful occasionally, but in my experience it is very difficult to lead a manufacturing plant while trying to act as the in-house Lean coach. The two roles of manufacturing manager and Lean coach require different skills and a different kind of relationship with the leadership team. Most companies consider the two approaches just described as a low-cost way to achieve improvement. In reality, even when this approach is successful (and in our experience it rarely is as successful as it can and should be), it takes much longer than engaging a dedicated Lean specialist. The cost of this delay to your improvement effort (the opportunity cost) can result in a considerable amount of lost savings, missed market opportunities, and loss of competitive advantage.

At TXM we recommend that SME manufacturers seek external Lean assistance from a specialist Lean consultant such as TXM. By employing a good Lean consultant, you are tapping into the expertise of individuals who have been trained in Lean techniques in major corporations such as Toyota and have implemented the Lean approach in dozens of companies. These specialists have a huge range of experience to call upon. Also important is that *when you engage Lean consultants, they will focus on one thing— improvements.* They are independent of the hierarchy and can work across and up and down the organization; they have a clear agenda and timeline to facilitate change.

Selecting a Lean Consultant

There are literally thousands of companies throughout the world that offer (or claim to offer) Lean manufacturing consulting services. I am told there are more than 6,000 in China alone! Unfortunately, there are no professional standards or registration bodies regulating consulting practices, so literally any consulting company without supporting credentials can—and frequently does—advertise as a "Lean consultant." The bottom line: You need to do your due diligence and choose with care. Factors to consider include

- What references does the consultant have? Can you visit some reference sites? Make sure you get some time alone with management at the reference site as some Lean consultants have been known to pass off the work of others as their own.
- What is the consultant's background? Lean is another term for the Toyota Production System, so therefore expect a strong connection to Toyota or the Toyota system (via training from ex-Toyota coaches).
- At TXM, we insist that our team members have some practical manufacturing experience, ideally in a manufacturing management role. Consultants with line experience know what it is like to meet daily delivery targets and deal with the multiple challenges of everyday life in a manufacturing plant. *Be wary of career consultants or trainers with little practical experience.* Even with consultants who have automotive assembly experience, make sure they have had some experience elsewhere in a manufacturing environment because an automotive assembly line is a unique environment, and consultants from that background may have trouble adapting to the realities of your process.
- Make sure you meet the consultants with whom you are going to work. The salesman or partner you meet might be very convincing but the

actual person who shows up on day one may be less so, so make sure you have met them and had some one-on-one time with each of them.

■ Training is not an effective way to drive change. Training is great to develop your employees and provide new skills, but in our experience *training programs do not drive change.* The way to achieve change is to focus on implementing Lean methods to achieve improvements. Learning occurs through making the change and applying Lean techniques to drive improved performance.

■ Avoid Lean Six Sigma. As explained in Chapter 1, I consider the Lean Six Sigma approach a highly bureaucratic, big-company approach that is not effective in SMEs.

I Need Someone Who Understands My Industry

The most common remark I get when meeting a prospective customer is, "My industry is unique. What experience do you have in my industry?" This is not a surprising question; I would ask it myself. However, in my years running a consulting business, I can say that, next to our expertise on Lean manufacturing, the greatest value we can bring to our customers is the insight we bring from our experience in other industries. When a prospective customer *insists* that the consultant knows that customer's industry, then he has significantly narrowed the available pool of consultants from which he can choose. Obviously, it is useful if the consultant knows the customer's industry because he or she will get up to speed a bit more quickly and will already know some of the jargon in the customer's business. On the other hand, I would consider a variety of industry experience as more important than knowledge of my industry alone. If you have two consultants who both meet all the criteria listed above, then perhaps the one who has some knowledge of your industry will have the edge, but personally I would put "industry knowledge" fairly low on the list of selection criteria.

However, there are some exceptions. A consultant with no technical or engineering training who has never worked in manufacturing is going to struggle in any manufacturing environment and will probably only be able to make superficial improvements. But if a consultant has practical manufacturing experience and is intelligent, he or she will quickly come to grips with the customer's industry and will bring new ideas the customer would never have gained from an industry specialist.

What about Hiring Your Own Internal Lean Consultants?

When considering the cost of a consultant, you may consider it better value to employ a full-time Lean specialist. On the face of it, this would seem like a great idea. I meet a lot of very frustrated Lean coordinators and Lean managers. Once you place such specialists within your organizational hierarchy, internal culture and structure place limits on what they can do. In our experience, *key line managers are often more willing to listen and take action when working with an external consultant who has been selected and appointed by the CEO than with an internal improvement person who is likely to be their junior.*

Do not allow that to stop you from developing internal Lean specialists; they will be necessary to carry on the message after the consultants leave. Our firm belief is that when you are starting out on your Lean journey, you are better off developing Lean specialists from within rather than hiring a high-powered expert from somewhere else, such as the automotive industry. If you choose well, your internal Lean specialist will have two things that the external hire will not have:

1. An excellent knowledge of your process
2. Existing relationships and the respect of the people in the organization

Your external Lean consultant can get the process rolling, influence the key leaders in the business with the support of the CEO, and develop the Lean skills of the nominated internal Lean specialists. In this way, the external consultant supports establishing the foundations of Lean manufacturing and breaking down the initial resistance to change. The internal team can then build on this foundation and drive further improvement.

The Branach Story…Continued from Chapter 1

At the beginning of this book, I told the story of Mike Walsh and his innovative ladder manufacturing business, Branach. Mike was typical of most manufacturing start-ups; he had designed a great product, found a ready market, grown his business, but had run into a big roadblock that prevented the further growth of his business—the performance of his factory.

Faced with this challenge in 2008, Mike engaged TXM to help him build a factory and manufacturing processes that could enable Branach to meet its full potential. My business partner, TXM Consulting Director Anthony Clyne, worked with Mike and his team over 12 months to implement almost all the systems and practices you have read in this book. We mapped the Branach value streams for extension ladders and A-frame access platforms (Chapter 4), developed load leveling to control the release of work and level production to *takt* time (Chapter 8). We helped Branach introduce first-in-first-out (FIFO) systems to manage the flow of work through the factory (Chapter 4). We developed a new factory layout (Chapter 6) and introduced *Kanban* systems, initially to manage the supply of internally made components and subassemblies, and later to manage the supply of all raw materials (Chapter 9). We introduced standard work to ensure products were manufactured in a consistent way and at a consistent rate (Chapter 11). We helped Mike develop an organizational structure that could support his key value streams (Chapter 6).

TXM Senior Consultant Michelle Brown coached Mike's front-line leaders and teams in the foundation skills of Lean, including 5S, problem solving, and daily leadership routines (Chapter 10). We then finally, in 2012, helped Mike relocate his now-fast-growing business to a new single site, removing the waste of moving materials back and forth across a public road.

The results have been spectacular. Lead times were reduced by up to 6 weeks. Branach can now provide next-day shipment for an access platform and around 4 days' lead time for a customized extension ladder. Productivity has increased approximately 30%, and the output of the ladder section assembly machine (which was previously the bottleneck) has more than doubled. As a result, Mike's business has doubled in sales with a minimal increase in overhead. He is now exporting his outstanding ladders to the Middle East, Europe, and the United States. The Branach team is now focusing on taking Lean to the next level with A3 planning, Lean design, and extending Lean beyond the factory floor and into the office. Just as Mike started his journey by visiting a factory to see Lean in action, he now frequently hosts visits from other SMEs hoping to learn from Branach's Lean journey. As for Mike himself, he is back doing what he loves and does best, designing the next generation of Branach ladders. Based on what I have seen, we can expect Branach to soon produce the lightest, strongest, and safest extension ladder ever made anywhere in the world—coming to a wall or a power pole near you. Figure 12.2 shows the Branach factory today.*

---

* To view an interview with Mike Walsh from Branach, go to http://txm.com.au/video/txm-video-lean-case-study-branach-manufacturing

Figure 12.2   Branach factory today.

Conclusion

This book is intended to be a starting point on your Lean manufacturing journey The purpose of this book is to provide a practical guide for operational managers and general managers in SMEs and get them started on their Lean mission.

I have provided many references and suggest that you purchase books on the topics of particular interest to you. Attend a conference or two; the Lean Enterprise Institute (LEI) and the Association for Manufacturing Excellence (AME) run regular conferences in a number of countries. I would always recommend these over the privately run conferences because with LEI and AME, you are going to the source and getting information from the originators of Lean manufacturing thinking. In fact, at LEI conferences you may get to hear from and meet some of the original Lean manufacturing gurus such as James Womack, Jeffrey Liker, and John Shook.

Finally, I would like you to congratulate yourself. If you have brought your manufacturing business to a point where you need Lean manufacturing help, it means that you have successfully established a business, developed products, developed a market for your products, grown your sales, and now need to improve your operational performance through Lean manufacturing methodologies to sustain this growth. It is a huge achievement to have traveled this far successfully, and many businesses will fail to get as far as yours has. It is easy to worry about the problems we face today and forget about the challenges we have already overcome and the ones we face tomorrow. There is no doubt you have a mountain to climb in order to implement Lean manufacturing. However, to establish and build your business, you have already climbed a much tougher mountain. Provided you show the same commitment and dedication to your Lean journey that you showed in starting and building your business, you can be almost certain of success.

Good luck in your Lean manufacturing journey!

Glossary of Lean Terms

5S: Workplace organization tool that standardizes a work area by

> **Sorting:** Leave only what is needed for the process.
>
> **Setting in order:** Arrange in the way you need it.
>
> **Shine:** Keep it clean and simple.
>
> **Standardizing:** Write the standards and share them.
>
> **Sustaining:** Audit, inspect, and improve the current standard—repeat.

A3 plan: An A3 plan is simply a business plan or project plan expressed on a single A3 sheet of paper. A3 plans are used for summarizing and explaining strategy (see also *Hoshin Kanri*), presenting projects, and solving problems. By limiting the format to a single A3 sheet of paper and applying rules around layout, A3 plans ensure that the essential information is communicated in a clear and concise fashion.

Andon: A visual feedback process that indicates a person has a problem in production or in part supply and needs assistance to fix the problem.

Continuous flow: One element of a JIT (just-in-time) system, continuous flow is where the production work-in-progress moves smoothly between work stages with little (or no) inventory buffers between each step.

ERP (Enterprise requirements planning): Today, ERP is used as a catch-all term to describe a wide range of business management software systems that link business operations with their financial recording. Most businesses will eventually need a business system of this type. However, these systems will include MRP planning tools (see below), also known as "push" scheduling, which is ineffective and should be avoided in most SMEs.

***Gemba*:** The place where value is actually created for the customer—the factory floor or workplace. To truly understand a situation, one needs to go to the *Gemba*, or the "real place," "the place where the truth can be found"—where work is done.

Heijunka **(Level scheduling):** A form of scheduling that is designed to manufacture smaller batches by sequencing a mix of product variants into the same product/process and leveling the rate of released work to production.

Hoshin Kanri **(Policy deployment):** *Hoshin Kanri* is the term used to describe the system used by Toyota to deploy its strategy through every level of its organization and also receive upward feedback on the strategy. *Hoshin Kanri* uses A3 plans to communicate strategy at each level.

Jidoka **(Autonomation):** Giving machines the ability to stop working when a defect or abnormal situation is automatically detected.

Just-in-Time (JIT): All production parts, consumables, and subassemblies are pulled into production according to customer demand, as opposed to the traditional "push" approach where parts are pushed in to production to meet expected future forecast demand using a central schedule or ERP/MRP system.

Kaizen **(Change for the better):** Applied to business organizations, it implies continuing improvement involving everyone. It usually refers to continuous small-step improvement over a sustained period of time. *Kaizen* usually happens at the *Gemba*, or workplace.

Kamishibai **(Red-green task board):** A system whereby colored "tee cards" are used to represent routine tasks in a workplace. In a typical application, the tags are printed red on one side and green on the other. They are then flipped from red to green as tasks are completed.

Kanban **(Pull system):** A process to signal the need for work, either for production to make something or stores, or supplier, to supply something. For *Kanban*, the signal is a physical indicator; it may be a card, an empty box, or a returned trolley.

Lean: A system of management based on the Toyota Production System that is focused on the relentless and ongoing elimination of waste or non-value-added time in order to reduce cost and capital while delivering maximum value to the customer.

MRP: Materials requirements planning—a software-driven process that plans the ordering of materials and scheduling of production based on forecasts. This is the basis of what is called "push" scheduling, where materials are "pushed" through a process to meet anticipated needs. This approach is not Lean and is particularly ineffective in SMEs (*see also* ERP).

***Muda* (Waste):** Waste—anything in the process that does not add value from the customer's perspective.

***Poka Yoke* (Error proofing):** Fixtures and methods in work design that prevent the creation of defects—they usually make it impossible to make a defect or clearly highlight a defect or abnormality in the process.

Toyota Production System: The management system and philosophy developed by Toyota and applied to its entire business since the 1950s.

Value stream map: Value stream mapping is a powerful Lean manufacturing technique used to document, analyze, and improve the flow of information or materials required to produce a product or service for a customer. Specifically, a "current state" value stream map identifies the value and waste in a process flow enabling development of a "future state map" to eliminate that waste.

Index